Gerald GOLDBERG

A TRIBUTE

Gerald GOLDBERG

A TRIBUTE

Edited by

Dermot Keogh and Diarmuid Whelan

MERCIER PRESS
WHAT YOU NEED TO READ

*To Fred Rosehill, Liz Steiner–Scott, the Cork Jewish community,
and in memory of Suzanne Crosbie.*

MERCIER PRESS

Cork

www.mercierpress.ie

Trade enquiries to CMD Distribution,

55A Spruce Avenue, Stillorgan Industrial Park,

Blackrock, County Dublin.

© Dermot Keogh, Diarmuid Whelan & Contributors, 2008

ISBN: 978 1 85635 581 0

10 9 8 7 6 5 4 3 2 1

A CIP record for this title is available from the British Library

Mercier Press receives financial assistance from the
Arts Council/An Chomhairle Ealaíon

Typeset by Dominic Carroll, Ardfield, Co. Cork

Printed and bound in the EU

Contents

Foreword

DERMOT KEOGH

The former president of University College, Cork, Professor Gerard Wrixon, approached me in 2002 to prepare a tribute to Gerald Yael Goldberg, solicitor, scholar, man of letters, intellectual, politician, patron of the arts and collector, and, not least, long-time leader of the Jewish community in Cork. Born in Cork in 1912, he died aged ninety-one on 31 January 2003 and was buried in the local Jewish graveyard. He was almost the last surviving member of the original local Jewish community. This collection of essays, in honour of one of Cork's most distinguished citizens, was slowly assembled over the intervening years. It was very fitting that Professor Wrixon, supported by the vice-president for planning, communications and development, Mr Michael O'Sullivan, should have persisted with the idea of a tribute to this outstanding public figure.

Gerald Goldberg had a lifelong association with his alma

mater, UCC. He had received an MA from UCC in 1968, and registered later to do a doctorate on representations of the Jew in the works of Shakespeare. He was awarded an honorary doctorate from UCC in 1993. His friendship with President Wrixon had grown over the years, as had his working relationship with the UCC librarian, John Fitzgerald, and myself. Gerald Goldberg left a considerable personal archive in the care of the college. It is now housed in the archives department of the library. The Goldberg donation contains the designs of many book covers for Penguin, Nonesuch Press and many other prestigious publishing houses. He was also the donor of a collection of letters, book designs, calligraphy and prints of the German artist Elizabeth Friedlander, who lived in Kinsale. In the light of his long association with UCC, it was appropriate that a tribute be paid in print to one of the university's most distinguished graduates.

Gerald Goldberg was born into an immigrant Jewish family. His father came from Lithuania and his mother was also of Lithuanian stock. His death, on 31 December 2003, occurred only a week before the hundredth anniversary of the disturbances in Limerick in 1904 when a mob attacked the homes of the small Jewish community – of which the Goldberg family were members – in Wolfe Tone Street. That event changed the lives of his parents and their older children. Although he had no personal memory of the event, having been born in 1912, his parents and older brothers and sisters could – and did – relate to him what had happened during those terrifying days. As a consequence, the Goldbergs moved to a Jewish community in Cork that was over 400 strong.

Happily, the independent Ireland in which Gerald Goldberg grew up – and to which his family contributed – reflected the ideals of tolerance and pluralism, albeit in an imperfect form

– ideals Gerald Goldberg strove in his lifetime to strengthen and reinforce as the guiding principles of Irish society. Educated at the Model School in Cork, he was also sent for a time by his father to a Jewish boarding school in Sussex. He attended Presentation College in Cork. Gerald Goldberg studied law at UCC and qualified as a solicitor in 1934. His legal studies, according to Professor David Gwynn Morgan, commenced in 1931 and began a long connection, cherished on both sides, where – through the years – Gerald Goldberg's 'idealism and legal skill were an inspiration to generations of law students'. When asked how he would describe Gerald Goldberg, the solicitor Jack Phelan chose the image of a diamond, renowned for its sparkle and for its cutting qualities. This is a man, he wrote in an essay for this volume, 'who shone at everything he did, student solicitor, husband, lord mayor – he shone as brightly as any diamond … the most precious of all gems.'

Gerald Goldberg married Sheila Smith in Belfast in the mid-1930s. They had three sons, David, Theo and John. Their home, Ben Truda, Douglas, became a gathering place for those interested in the arts, literature, the law and cultural life. Both Gerald and Sheila were deeply involved with the Cork Orchestral Society, Irish ballet and the staging of musical events in the city.

Gerald Goldberg was elected an alderman of Cork Corporation in 1967, and he became the first Jewish lord mayor of Cork in 1977. He told the journalist, Dick Hogan: 'I have always loved Cork. As a Jew, and as one who grew up and made my career here, I believed that people like me owed something to the State, that we should give something back to the places in which we were spawned. That is why I stayed and that is why I consider myself to be a proud son of Cork. I have no recriminations. My city elected me as its first citizen, the National University of Ireland conferred me with an honorary degree. I love my city, my faith and my Irishness,' he said.

As lord mayor, he went on an official visit to the United States, where he was given the freedom of a number of cities, including New York and Philadelphia. (At the auction of the contents of his house following his death, I bought a number of books autographed by the mayors of the different cities. Mayor Ed Koch of New York was one of those who wrote a dedication to him.)

Gerald Goldberg is remembered in his native city as a determined leader of the Jewish community in Cork, as a distinguished scholar-practitioner of law, as an intellectual, as a writer, as a collector and as a patron of the arts, and as a man of local politics and of public affairs. His Jewish faith was a driving force in his life, as also was the central importance of education. These gave a focus to his lifetime of service to his community and to his country. He enriched the lives of many generations of people in his native city and in the country.

His life spanned the twentieth century – correctly described as the 'century of extremes', but a somewhat inadequate phrase when referring to the century in which the Holocaust occurred. He held a lingering, profound disappointment at the inadequate response of the Irish government during the Second World War to the European refugee crises. But as an Irishman, he served between 1939 and 1945 as a part-time soldier in the army, ready to defend his country.

Towards the end of his life, he had a major regret about the decline of the Cork Jewish community. He told Dick Hogan: 'I am resentful of the decline and resentful of the fact that what is left of the Jewish community in Cork has been neglected by their fellow Jews, particularly in Dublin. It's too late now for a revival. I don't see it happening, the opportunity for that has come and gone. I'm the oldest Jew left in Cork. What has happened here is nothing short of heartbreaking. It is one of the greatest sadnesses in my life.'

On a personal note, I associate Gerald Goldberg with great generosity of spirit. He was prepared to share his knowledge, his experience, his wisdom, his books and his archives with students and teachers alike. He had a very wide and deep knowledge of history, of literature, of the visual and performing arts, and of Judaism. His eloquence and his wisdom will live on because he was, in a single word, a rabbi – that is, a teacher.

I am grateful to all those who so generously agreed to contribute to this volume. I am also thankful for their patience and, ultimately, their faith that this book would see the light of day. This is due in great measure to my colleague, Dr Diarmuid Whelan, who helped bring the text to finality. My thanks to Eileen O'Carroll, who helped sub-edit the text and gave many useful suggestions. Charlotte Holland helped type part of the text. Anne Kearney and the late Suzanne Crosbie of the *Irish Examiner* and Carol Quinn of the Boole Library, UCC were generous with their time in sourcing photographs. Mary Feehan and Brian Ronan in Mercier Press were most supportive throughout.

The publication of this volume was generously supported by funds provided through the vice-president for planning, communications and development, Michael O'Sullivan.

My thanks to Gerald Goldberg's family, with a special mention for Theo, who provided so much assistance with photos. Their help and support for the publication of this volume was most encouraging. Mr Fred Rosehill, the leader of the Cork Jewish community, greatly supported this project and provided expert advice and assistance over the past few years.

My Uncle

DAVID MARCUS

Once upon a time I had an uncle who frequently 'cheated'! He was the youngest of my mother's five brothers and he was my favourite, my uncle Gerald, because although I was only a kid and he was, to me, already an old man of twenty, he never refused to play games with me. It made no difference what the game was – cricket, soccer, table tennis, draughts, ludo, donkey – indoor, outdoor, against the wall, on the table, under the table – he was ever-ready, willing and as tireless as I was. But I soon began to suspect that he often beat me by 'cheating'.

At first I couldn't believe that I was right. When I'd bowl to him at cricket and the ball would beat his bat only to be kept out of the stumps by his broad leg, I'd should 'Howzat' gleefully and run to dispossess him. But 'No,' he'd protest, 'never out. I was miles outside the wicket. Look!' And I'd look, and sure enough his leg would be where he said I'd find it and not where I thought I'd seen it. It must have been the angle, I'd tell myself – and I'd turn to pick up the ball.

Or at snakes-and-ladders he'd quickly pop the dice back into the cup just before I could be certain it was a two he had thrown and not the six he claimed, and I'd conclude that it must all have been an optical illusion.

Not for long, however. After all, there was a limit even to my gullibility, and soon I had no possible doubt about what was going on. But what to do about it? Dared I be so presumptuous as to accuse him to his face of actually cheating? My father would surely give me a smacking if he knew. And if he didn't know, my uncle himself might well do likewise – or worse still, refuse to play with me again. But how could I win if he continued to cheat? I suffered silently for ages, running up the greatest consecutive losing sequence in the history of family sports.

Came the day when I could no longer contain myself. I don't remember what the game was – but that hardly matters – because I just suddenly burst out, 'But you're cheating, uncle Gerald, really cheating.'

He looked at me, eyes widening with amazement. 'Of course,' he said calmly, 'I always try to cheat you because it's only a game, and I wondered how long before you'd learn to stand up for yourself. You see, playing a game is entertainment, and so our games are just fun. But you're old enough now to learn that even though they're fun, they are also a part of life that has rules just as real life has. Real-life rules are what you must live by. Learn that, Dovidil [his favourite Hebrew name for me], and always think of it. If you do, I won't be able to cheat you again, will I?'

Well, that was a mouthful of a moral and philosophical poser for a kid having the first real think of his life. I imagine that uncle Gerald very soon forgot the story of the first life-experience lesson he taught me, but I always remembered it.

A Man of Many Talents

JACK PHELAN

A diamond has certain characteristics. A diamond sparkles, brilliantly; a diamond has many faces or, if you prefer, aspects; a diamond is – as that film claimed – forever, and, most importantly, a diamond is renowned for its cutting qualities. If this writer was asked to use just one word to describe Gerald Goldberg, 'diamond' is the word that would spring to mind.

Gerald Goldberg, whether in his office or in court, sparkled (as can be testified from many a hard-fought court battle, Gerald Goldberg was renowned and is remembered for his cutting edge.) Like the diamond, he had many faces: he was a lawyer, a politician, an art lover, a patron of music, a leading light in Cork's Jewish community, a part-time soldier in the 1939–45 Emergency; and, most importantly of all, a lord mayor and as such First Citizen of the city of Cork.

But who was he? How did he come to be in Cork? What made him a lawyer? How did he become Cork's First Citizen? All these are interesting questions, and all have interesting answers.

Gerald Goldberg's parents were from Lithuania, a country now independent and free, but at the turn of the twentieth century a place dominated by Russia. The subject of disputes with Germany, it was not a good place for Jews to be, even though Jewish people had lived there for centuries. America beckoned for many, and the Goldbergs decided that America was the destination to which they would emigrate. Just like the Irish, emigrants from the Baltic states had to travel by the cheapest method possible: not quite the coffin ships of Irish history but still by the most basic sea transport. Going ashore at what they were told was the 'next parish to New York', they found that this was true – kind of – but that the stretch of water separating Ireland from New York was a little too wide to cross in a day. So after some twists and turns, the Goldberg parents settled in Ireland.

Ireland in those days was still governed from London by a parliament that, frankly, did not, like Mr Rhett Butler, give a damn about Ireland, and especially its problems. The Goldberg parents moved to Limerick and were happy there, but fled that city when there occurred what was perhaps Ireland's only Jewish pogrom, which was confined to Limerick and fuelled by the actions of a misguided priest.

So Gerald Goldberg as a young boy found himself a Corkonian, and although he should have been in America – had his parents' original ambition been realised – he stayed, studied and prospered. Apart from a very short stay in an English school, he was educated in the Presentation Brothers College in Cork and went on to University College, Cork, where he studied law.

Gerald was a bit different from some of the other Irish Jews, as it was more usual at that time for Jewish boys to go to Trinity College in Dublin; indeed, Wesley College on Stephen's Green was where most of his co-religionists attended for their secondary education. But Gerald Goldberg had already – like an uncut diamond – a certain sparkle.

Following his days at UCC, Gerald was apprenticed to a Cork solicitor. Nowadays, the term 'apprentice' has fallen out of favour in the corridors of the Law Society, and young people who aspire to be solicitors are encouraged to call themselves 'trainee solicitors' – which, in my opinion, they are not. Equally, the well-respected term 'masters' for solicitors taking apprentices is frowned upon, and the authorities want to use the awful label 'training solicitors', conjuring up, for this writer at least, a spectacle of young law students galloping around a courtroom being schooled by a trainer in the manner of young racehorses. Suffice it to say that Gerald Y. Goldberg served his apprenticeship, passed the required examinations of the Law Society, and was admitted a solicitor in 1936.

He did not join a firm as an assistant with hopes of being made a partner in due course, but set up on his own right from the start. Since his parents were not in the legal profession, there was no family firm to keep a seat warm for the new boy, so it was a case of 'plunge in at the deep end and start swimming'.

Very soon, Goldberg was being talked of in Cork's then rather limited and confined legal circles. He began to make a name for himself representing the many poor people who then, as now, were before the courts for a multitude of offences. Because he was a solicitor and not a barrister, his principal advocacy was in the District Court; his reputation as a practitioner in that arena was very soon established and spread far beyond Cork city and county. In theory, a solicitor also had a right of audience in the Circuit Court – not so, of course, in the High Court or in the Supreme Court – and he did so with good effect. (At the time, and indeed right up to very recently, a solicitor who represented a client in the Circuit Court without briefing a barrister would very quickly be given short shrift by whatever learned Circuit judge the foolish solicitor appeared before.) But in legal circles, if one wants to be a solicitor, one must have an office, and if one has an office, one has to be in that office, so the dilemma arises for the sole or single practitioner: how to be a great court advocate and yet be the manager of an office and meet the public at the same time. Being realistic, Gerald Goldberg did as many others in law had done before him: he became an outstanding practitioner in the District Court, specialising in representing clients in civil cases. The people who would never have gone to the bigger 'family' offices went to him, and where their cases merited being brought in the Circuit or High Court, he issued proceedings on their behalf, briefed barristers to appear when the cases were being heard, and all the time prepared those cases with meticulous care and deadly accuracy.

He never, however, turned away from those who needed his services in the criminal courts, and gave the same care to criminal cases whatever the nature of the alleged offence or crime. Over the years his name became synonymous with many of Cork's most famous murder trials – in one much-talked-of trial, following an acquittal the accused man was carried out triumphant on his friends' shoulders. There were many who felt that it was Gerald Goldberg who should have been the person shouldered out.

For many years the office of Gerald Goldberg was situated at Library House on the corner of Pembroke Street and South Mall. Previously, the 'Cork Library', dating from the eighteenth century, was situated here, and the words 'Cork Library' can still be seen high upon the building. Then the office moved to above the Burton buildings adjoining Patrick Street. Partners in law have come and gone, but until he retired, Gerald Y. Goldberg – or 'Goldie', as some of us fondly referred to him – was always the principal.

Sadly, he never became a judge. Until very recently, solicitors could only become District judges; much too late, the position of Circuit judge was opened to the profession, and only in 2002 could solicitors become eligible to be appointed judges of the High Court. With so much experience of law and advocacy, Goldberg would have made a very good judge.

Controversy dogged his relationship with the Southern Law Association (SLA), the governing body of Cork city's solicitors. In his time, Gerald had served on the council of the SLA and became vice-president. Normally, the vice-president becomes president the following year. There is one caveat – to be president one must be a member of the council, and under SLA rules all council members retire each year and an election is held among the members for council. In the year of his vice-presidency, Gerald Goldberg, with all other council members, retired and sought re-election. To the surprise of many – and to the bitter disappointment of Mr Goldberg – he was not re-elected to the council, so could not be president. Gerald Y. Goldberg resigned his membership of the Southern Law Association, and relations became very strained. Honest as ever, he believed that he had not been re-elected because he was a Jew, but others in the profession say this was not so.

This unhappy rift existed for many years, but on the occasion of Judge John Clifford's retirement from the Circuit Court in

2002, SLA president Patrick Dorgan had his council invite Mr Goldberg and a number of other long-serving solicitors to be the association's guests at a lunch to mark the judge's retirement. Gerald Goldberg accepted the invitation, and the president paid special tribute to the special guests, a tribute that brought sustained applause from the very large attendance.

Later on, he went back to UCC, his beloved university, and became a student again. He graduated with an MA, adding it to his LLB. Indeed it can be argued that he is probably one of the college's most exalted legal graduates.

Another of those interesting questions: how did Gerald Goldberg become lord mayor of Cork? From an early stage, the Goldberg family were strong supporters of Irish independence, so it was no surprise that the young solicitor interested himself in politics. He was first elected to Cork Corporation as an independent, and established his reputation in City Hall as a fearless advocate of Cork and of the weak.

Sometimes, being an independent in a party-political structure can be an advantage, but on the Corporation, such independence cuts little ice. Ever a realist, Gerald Goldberg became a member of Fianna Fáil, and eventually became lord mayor. The people of Cork, of all political persuasions and religions, still speak of the manner in which our first Jewish lord mayor discharged his duties. It is perhaps a tribute to Ireland's Jewish community that the names of Briscoe and Goldberg will be forever spoken of when outstanding lord mayors are mentioned: Briscoe in Dublin and Goldberg in Cork.

If there is one matter of political business unfinished then it is the failure of Fianna Fáil to nominate Gerald Y. Goldberg as a member of the Seanad. The Dáil is elected by vote of the people; it is party political and meant to be: that is our system. Seanad Éireann was meant to be a chamber of all that was best in Ireland and *for* Ireland. Gerald Goldberg would have been a great member of the Seanad had he been nominated to that chamber.

When the Second World War began, Goldberg joined the Local Defence Force – the LDF of fond memory. He enjoyed his time in that force; he is reported to have said that he was good at marching but a very poor marksman. He was one of the very few members of the LDF marked down for arrest and execution by the Nazis when, as they believed, 'Der Tag' would come and Germany would, having conquered Britain, disregard our neutrality and arrive in Ireland to institute their thousand-year rule. Fortunately, 'Der Tag' and the Nazis never arrived.

At the start of the war, as befitting a member of Ireland's Jewish community, Gerald Goldberg hoped for the admission to Ireland of a sizable number of Jewish refugees fleeing Nazi oppression. Sadly, although some refugees did find shelter in this country, an official policy of limiting numbers meant that many people who could have been accommodated here were disappointed; how many who were refused and who subsequently died in concentration camps can only be a matter of conjecture and shame.

What of Goldberg the man? Was he just a great solicitor and lord mayor? No, not at all. When Gerald was a young man, he went to Belfast with members of the Boy Scouts. There he met an attractive lady, and by great fortune a member of Belfast's Jewish community. Sheila Smith soon became 'Mrs. G.Y.G.' and came to Cork, where they raised three sons. When her husband became lord mayor, the new lady mayoress threw herself into her position with the zest she brought to all her previous activities. Gerald and

Sheila instituted a series of lunchtime concerts, in furtherance of their roles as patrons of art and artists.

To conclude, it is usual when reviewing the career of those who have shone in their professions to say that the person being discussed was an 'ornament' to their profession. To me, an ornament conjures up a vision of something nice but of no practical value. Gerald Y. Goldberg was no ornament. This is a man who shone at everything he did: student, solicitor, husband, lord mayor. He shone as brightly as any diamond. Indeed, I'll finish as I started – a diamond sparkles and Gerald Y. Goldberg sparkled with the brilliant clear light of a diamond, the most precious of all gems.

A Man for All Seasons

MARY BANOTTI

It was a Sunday in January 1971. I had returned to Ireland after fourteen years racketing around the world, and was visiting my uncle, Seán Collins, the former deputy from Roaringwater Bay. 'We are going over for coffee to visit the Duchess and Gerald.' I knew no one in Ireland after my long absence, and was looking forward to meeting a real duchess. And she was – not just a duchess but a queen. Sheila Goldberg: Belfast woman, sister of Sydney Smith (a wonderful artist), married to G.Y., a woman of great charm, infinite grace, a truly wicked sense of humour, and a loyal and loving wife and mother. The uncle, who had a legendary orator's voice, dominated that first meeting, but it was the commencement of one of the greatest and most important friendships of my life.

Straight away I was engulfed in the aroma of rich coffee and delicious homemade cakes and, above all, wonderful conversation and loving friendship. Gerald told me of his memories as a small boy listening to Michael Collins speaking in Cork. That was the start of a lifelong love and respect for the Collins history. He painted a picture of a small boy in an immigrant Jewish family with vivid memories of the Limerick pogrom. He took me to see the house where he had grown up. It was through Gerald's eyes that I learned what it was to have a passionate love affair with a city. That great love existed until the end. I always seemed to know that his great wish was to be lord mayor of Cork, and I was lucky to see him and Sheila invested as the First Citizens of their city. We have lovely pictures of us all standing in City Hall in Cork with Gerald and Sheila in their ceremonial robes, the ever-present twinkle in both their eyes.

For over thirty years I was welcomed warmly into the Goldberg home. When I worked in Irish Distillers in Cork, I generally visited once or twice a month. To visit Gerald and Sheila was to enter an Aladdin's cave of experiences. I learned a great deal about the best of Irish artists by looking at their collections. I learned the great histories and traditions of Irish glass. I had the pleasure of touching work from some of the great sculptors. Every year, there was something new and wonderful to discover in the garden, one of Sheila's great passions. But above all, there was always Gerald's conversation about the latest book he was reading, articles in the *New York Review of Books*, the *Irish Times* or the *Cork Examiner*. Talks centring on another of his great passions and the basis of his university thesis – Judaic references in Shakespeare – were a history lesson in themselves. Gerald had meticulous, small handwriting, and I find in my box of letters little notes that accompanied books he sent me. He introduced me to Francis Stewart, Elizabeth Bowen, Honor Tracy, James Joyce, the calligraphy of Eric Gill and Elizabeth Friedlander, and the history of the Jews in Ireland. The list is endless.

It wasn't just reading the book that was important: with Gerald and these writers, one benefited from talking with someone who had both personal friendships with these writers or a sharp psychological contact with them. When talking about them, Gerald would lean back in his seat and a look of pure pleasure would suffuse his face. Music had the same effect on him, and I remember being signalled to stop talking to listen to some particularly exquisite movements from Mahler. Every time I left 'Ben Truda', I felt I left with a wonderful present that would always enhance my life.

There were shadows of course. Gerald changed his political colours and I challenged him on this – but in the best of good humour. When I ran for the Seanad in 1983, he promised me his number-one and gave it to me. As I sat at the Seanad count, behind me stood Mr Justice Seán O'Leary. Being totally inexperienced politically at the time, I thought he was there to congratulate me on winning. But no, he was there to see where my number-twos were going. A vote came up – no. 1: Banotti, no. 2: Martin O'Donoghue – and Mr. Justice O'Leary began to whistle 'On the Banks of My Own Lovely Lee'! There is no doubt about it: the Irish political system is totally transparent.

The deepest shadow was the passing of our beloved Sheila. When her health began to deteriorate, and even in her darkest hour, there always remained traces of that wicked, delicious sense of humour. I visited her regularly in the nursing home in Blackrock. Gerald spent two years of constant daily visits, and established warm and supportive friendships with the staff in that lovely place. She died when I was in Strasbourg, and I was indeed fortunate to arrive in Cork in time for her funeral. Those who stood on the side of the hill of the Jewish cemetery in Cork represented all that was best in the life of Cork and in the cultural life of our country. On the way to the cemetery, she was given the honour of the flags on City Hall flying at half-mast. We stood on the steps to salute her as the cortege passed by; she would have loved that, and she richly deserved it.

She had been a founder member of Abode, and a great supporter with Gerald of the School of Music and the Crawford Art Gallery. All of them had benefited from her love and patronage. I still can't think of her without missing her and shedding a little tear. After Sheila died, we worried about Gerald's capacity to survive without her. But he was a person of huge personal resources, and was blessed to be surrounded by caring friends and excellent neighbours. The house was still a place of wonder and delight. Gerald would still greet you with a flirtatious and naughty air – he was a bit of a divil – thank goodness!

If I have not spoken about him as a lawyer, it is because that was a part of his life I knew little about, though I know it was through his long service in Cork that he was known across all social and cultural levels. The expression 'going down to see Goldberg' was part of the life of the city when troubles struck. His courtly manner and great knowledge of the law must have been a huge comfort for many people standing in front of His Lordship.

I am pleased and honoured to recall my memories of one of the most unforgettable and distinguished citizens of this country. We will not see his likes again.

'Appeal at once'

FRED ROSEHILL

Gerald Yael Goldberg, or GY as he was known to the Jewish community in Cork, first burst on the communal scene in October 1943 when he was elected President of the Cork Hebrew Congregation. For the following sixty years, GY was the public face of Cork Jewry, and involved himself in every facet of communal life.

Spiritual leaders had to be maintained, Kosher food had to be provided, the Jewish cemetery had to be kept in proper condition, a Hebrew school supported – and it fell to the people of the community to assist in all those services to make them function.

Communal politics existed, the older generation did not see things change easily, and the long-gone communal buildings of no. 9 South Terrace echoed to the sounds of protests and ire on a Sunday morning where the meetings of the community were held.

Gerald Goldberg was very well versed in Jewish religious life, and was able to act as a cantor when the occasion required. He taught young people in the Hebrew school when a teacher was not available.

Gerald championed debates and lectures in our social club. His love of sport of all codes was well known, and even in later years he turned out as a goalie in the local Jewish football team.

Gerald Y. Goldberg was a very proud Corkman; whether it was in defence of his city, his religion or his country, he gave to all with extreme passion. His contribution to his community was immeasurable and served as a example to those who followed him. In challenging the old attitudes, he succeeded in putting a public face on Cork Jewry for the first time in its history.

In the 1940s, when the Jewish world was in chaos in Europe and the isolation of the Cork Jewish community from the Jewish world became obvious, GY sought to tighten the bond with its nearest Irish community, in Dublin. Alas, his efforts did not succeed and, to show his displeasure, on 17 April 1947 he withdrew the Cork representative from the Representative Council of Ireland.

He did not suffer fools gladly.

In conclusion, let me recall one of Goldberg's favourite quotes: 'No man can be a sound lawyer who is not well versed in the laws of Moses.' He had a very good sense of humour. On one occasion, I sent him a message from the court to the Jewish Council: 'Justice has prevailed.' Goldberg wired back, 'Appeal at once!'

Three Unjustly Uncelebrated Local-government Cases

DAVID GWYNN MORGAN

MAN OF LAW

It is in every way fitting that the oldest-serving member of the university's law department should be allowed the honour of writing a chapter in a book devoted to its most distinguished son. Gerald Goldberg's connection with the department was long and, I think, cherished on both sides. It commenced when he came here in 1931, as one of a group of students literally in single figures who entered that year (times change: 155 students entered in 2008).

His idealism and legal skill were inspirational to generations of law students; for he was one of a select group of scholar-practitioners – one thinks also of his peers, the part-time Professors

Ted Ryan and Bryan Murphy – who kept vital and bright the links between the department and the practising professions. Gerald was always ready to give a lecture to our day or evening students, which ranged over wide fields of legal practice, and brought together his zeal for justice in practice and the principles of jurisprudence in a very real and vivid way. In 1993, Gerald brought great honour on the department and the university when he was awarded an honorary LL D – seldom have the honour and graduand been more well matched.

Gerald Goldberg was of course a Renaissance man, and I know that attempts, no doubt well-intentioned, are being made elsewhere in this volume to annex him to the cause of literature, theology, local government and goodness knows what else. He certainly contributed more in these areas than most who laboured only in these fields, but first of all he belonged to the tribe of lawyers and, in particular, to the breed of solicitor – indeed, the best-known solicitor in Cork and a name to conjure with in many a northside sketch from 'The Swans'.[1] His learning, far-sightedness and resourcefulness were poured out in unstinting libations for his clients. Somehow, one is reminded of the relief that Gerald Goldberg's very name could bring to his clients by the title of the memoirs of another great Jewish solicitor, Lord Goodman; his autobiography was called *Tell Them I'm On My Way*.[2]

Gerald had all the rugged individualism and integrity of the best kind of solicitor. Not for them the courtly Latin of 'me learned friends' in the High Court. As Bryan Murphy, part-time professor in the Law Department and colleague of Gerald's on the South Mall, once remarked to the present writer: 'The solicitor who goes down a sewer to take a good statement from a witness is doing more for his client than all the counsel in Creation.' I think that

Gerald would approve that remark. The solicitor has to stand for his client against landlord, employer, spouse or the insolence of office, and at a criminal trial he was always prepared to stand between his client – certainly uneducated, possibly illiterate – and the organised power of the state, and to see to it that if the prosecution were to convict, it would have to prove its case beyond reasonable doubt. He gave reality to this principle, which has been called the 'golden thread' running through our criminal-justice system.

Gerald's companion and support was his wife Sheila, an independent woman, who made a great success of her year as Lady Mayoress.

THE BACKGROUND

We turn now to three cases which are not as well known as they should be to academicians, though they are part of the rich lore of local government known to councillors, administrators and law agents, who are, perhaps, too busy to write about them.

In the first editorial of the revived *Irish Jurist*, the patriarch of Irish public law, J.M. Kelly, uncharacteristically made a mistake. Writing in 1966, Professor Kelly stated that:

Presumably when the legislature creates administrative powers, it must be taken to intend these powers to be used with fairness and reasonableness so that, in a sense, the law is broken whenever such powers are used otherwise; but the truth seems to be that provided an authority entrusted with administrative discretion keeps inside its *vires* and (where appropriate) commits no open breach of natural justice it may act as foolishly, unreasonably or even unfairly as it likes and the Courts cannot (or at any rate will not) interfere.[3]

Commenting on this statement only a few years later, the same writer made *amende honorable*:

> In the light of four subsequent Irish decisions, it is clear that this point of view, whatever justification it may have had in 1966, does not now correctly state Irish law on the matter; … the Courts have, within the last three years, explicitly marked out bridgeheads from which the exercise of statutory discretion can be controlled on more penetrating criteria than mere vires (as traditionally understood) or natural Justice.[4]

However, the significant point is that the judicial review of administrative action, though by no means the torrent which it has become, did not begin in or around 1966.[5] In fact, there has been for several centuries a framework of precedents to bind in the mighty leviathan of the state. Three of these earlier authorities (only one of them a member of Professor Kelly's quartet) dealing with bad faith (*mala fides*) remain of interest today, not least because Gerald was the solicitor for the applicant in the earliest of them.

By way of setting these cases in context, one should say that the bloc of law of which they form part – judicial review of administrative action – applies where an administrative agency – it may be a minister or a local authority or a regulatory body – is given a statutory power. In the modern administrative state, there will be thousands of such powers dealing both with what the state, or its agencies, does directly itself and with its interventions in the businesses or other activities of its citizens. To take almost random examples, these powers may operate in such areas as welfare benefits, tax collection, immigration, trade licensing, planning control or standard setting for health and safety at work.

The law devised and operated by the courts, in what for them is a rather alien field, is the product of two tensions. On the one hand, the judges should not operate such close control as in effect to substitute the view of a judge for that of a public administrator; that may be undesirable for all kinds of reasons, not least that here judges do not always know best. On the other hand, the administrative authority must not be allowed to go completely berserk. The resolution of these two tensions is that judicial review is concerned not directly with the merits of a decision but with certain 'up-stream' aspects that make up the concept of legality. Put briefly, there are three segments to this concept: the administrative agency must observe the limits (or *vires*) set in the legislation itself (for instance, if the legislature has authorised the Employment Appeals Tribunal to order only the payment of compensation, it may not order reinstatement); secondly, the administrative agency must follow the rules of fair procedure (constitutional justice) which – the law assumes – will be likely to lead on to a just result; finally, the administrative agency must not act in an unreasonable or arbitrary fashion. The way in which this last head as to unreasonableness has been cast has varied somewhat in scope and jargon (with the Constitution, even now, playing a surprisingly small role). But one can say that, in essence, it consists of the following features: the power must be exercised in good faith; taking relevant factors into account and neglecting unreasonable factors; and reasonably.

What, then, is bad faith, which was at the centre of the three cases under review here? Bad faith (frequently known as '*mala fides*' or fraud) exists where a public body intends to achieve an object other than that for which it believes the power to have been conferred.

THREE UNJUSTLY UNCELEBRATED CASES

The calibre of Gerald Goldberg was never better displayed than in the case of *The State (O'Mahony) vs. South Cork Board of Public Health* [1941] Ir. Jur. Rep. 79. Seen with the eye of the time, one can perceive his remarkable quality. In the early 1940s, in an age of deference, he stood up for a humble Corkonian against the might of the county borough council. 'Don't buck City Hall!' was a precept he disdained.

The case with which we are mainly concerned was heard by a divisional High Court (of Maguire P., Hanna J. and Maguire J.) on 23–24 April 1941 at a time when Gerald, Mrs O'Mahony's solicitor, had been admitted for only three years. The applicant, Mrs Rose O'Mahony 'of Skehard, Blackrock in the county of Cork' (as the report puts it, reflecting the spacious days when there were green fields between Blackrock and Cork city), was a tenant of the South Cork Board of Public Health. A little earlier, the Labourers Act 1936, section 16 had enacted a tenant-purchase scheme, benefiting tenants of cottages held under the Labourers Acts and putting them in a position largely equivalent to that of tenants of agricultural holdings under the historic nineteenth-century Land Acts. Unfortunately, there had been bad blood between the parties for some time. According to Maguire P., who gave judgment for the court:

> During the year 1940 certain difficulties arose out of that very fertile source of trouble between landlords and tenants, viz the obligation to repair. In this case we find the usual position reversed. The obligation to repair rested on the landlords. The applicant was active in carrying out repairs to the cottage and had sought to make the respondents responsible for the

expense of repairs which she claimed to have done by reason of the default of the respondents. In this she was partially successful ... obtaining a [High Court] decree against them for £18 in respect of these repairs.

The reason why the last sentence says that the applicant was partially successful was that she had in fact claimed £36. The sum of £18 is the equivalent of €1,000 in today's values, and one must allow for the fact that builders were less well paid, even in real terms, in those days.

The response of the board was swift. On 9 March 1940 a notice to quit was served on Mrs O'Mahony; it expired on 17 March. A summons for possession was served on 20 March. On 27 March an application from Mrs O'Mahony, completed by Gerald, was served, setting out her claim to purchase under the 1936 Act on the basis that she was the tenant of the cottage. But this application was rejected on 15 April. Judicial review proceedings followed with, by today's standards, remarkable celerity, the conditional order being obtained on 15 November 1940 and the substantive hearing taking place six months later.

The board's initial feint was founded on the fact that it had secured a decree for possession, which had not, however, been executed. This thrust the court rejected with some hauteur, on the basis that, given the purpose of the Act, 'it seems strange that the board should be entitled to determine the tenancy without very grave reason. I am doubtful if they were entitled to do so save on grounds which would entitle them to refuse her application to be allowed to purchase.' And even if this were not so, the fact the notice to quit had expired did not prevent her possession amounting to occupation within the statute.

The ground thus cleared, Maguire P. turned to the main point of principle, and held that

> Reading between the lines of the affidavits, it would appear that the Board was annoyed because she had taken on herself to do repairs to her cottage and more annoyed still because she had obtained a decree against them for £18 in respect of these repairs ... Mere pique at an unfavourable judgment in the High Court seems to me to be no justification for attempting to deprive the applicant of her legal rights ... The Board of Health have failed to consider her application. This Court must direct the Board to reconsider it.[6]

The second case, this time in the Midlands, also centred on the right to purchase under the Labourers Act. In *The State (McGeough) vs. Louth County Council* 1071LT (1973) 13, the applicant had purchased the cottage under the Act. By the time of the case (being seventy-four years old and unable to live alone any longer), she needed to go to live with her grandniece; she wished, therefore, to sell her cottage. But under the Act, she had to have the consent of the local authority. The county manager had refused consent, as he had on the thirteen other occasions on which consent had been sought by tenant-purchasers. In this, he was fortified by the following unanimous resolution of the county council: 'We the members of the Louth County Council refuse to consent to the sale of any more cottages.'

The eight judges (three in the High Court, five in the Supreme Court) who heard the case, each giving a written judgment, found it hard to contain their indignation that so many rules of administrative law should have been broken at one time, over one small cottage. In the first place, the county manager was acting contrary to the policy of the Act and was probably doing so in bad faith. He had, unfortunately, left himself open to the suggestion that his attitude towards applications for consent to sell had been 'arbitrary, capricious and obstructive' (Kingsmill Moore J.). Maguire C.J. went on to put a related point:

> In my view, however, it was not intended by the requirement of consent to enable the county manager to impose conditions other than or at variance with those which are so clearly set out in the Act. Consent may justifiably be refused because the proposed purchaser is not an agricultural labourer, as was the case here. There may be other reasons but they must be connected with the non-fulfilment of statutory conditions. There can be no general policy in relation to the giving or refusal of consent. Each individual case must be considered separately.

The next issue covered the council resolution against giving consent. The matter was outside the councillors' jurisdiction and the manager should not have allowed himself to be influenced by it. As was said succinctly by Ó Dálaigh J.: 'The resolution should never have been passed. Having been passed, it should have been promptly rescinded. Not having been rescinded, it should have been ignored.'

The final point has a strikingly contemporary ring to it. That pioneering public law judge, Kingsmill Moore J., stated: 'I think also that the owner is entitled to be informed, at least in general terms, as to why the consent has been refused, so that he may be able to meet any objections to the granting of consent.'

As a third example of a solicitor (another UCC law graduate,

Robert Pierse) in a small town who was prepared to bring a case that involved accusing councillors of bad faith, take *Listowel UDC vs. McDonagh* [1968] IR 312. The basis of the case, this time, was the Local Government (Sanitary Services) Act 1948, by which a sanitary authority is empowered: '[to] prohibit the erection of … temporary dwellings … if they be of opinion that such erection … would be prejudicial to public health'. Purporting to act on the ground of public health, Listowel UDC made an order banning the parking of caravans on a number of named streets. The defendant, who was an itinerant, was convicted and fined ten shillings in the High Court for contravening this order. Though the amount was low, the issue of principle was high, recalling John Hampden's remark during the turbulent years leading up to the English Civil War when King Charles I sought to levy 'ship money' (an illegitimate tax the king sought to impose so as to avoid having to summon parliament). The amount levied against John Hampden's land was deliberately kept low in the hope that he would not protest. The hope was dashed, with Hampden remarking: 'If they can take 30 shillings, they can take all I have.'

The accused's principal line of defence was to argue that the order had not been made bona fide, in that the sanitary authority did not genuinely hold the necessary opinion. Once again, there was a sub-plot, in this case a sophisticated, even esoteric, point. The prosecution submitted that the claim of bad faith could only be heard in judicial-review proceedings; they could not be made in collateral proceedings, such as, in the instant case, a criminal prosecution. The Supreme Court rejected this argument.

On the main point, the Supreme Court ruled that *mala fides* is 'a well recognised ground of challenge', and that the defendant was free to adduce evidence as to what transpired at the council meeting that considered the passing of the bye-law; what views were expressed by members and officials of the council; and the veracity of the opinion they expressed. In the result, the case was returned to the Circuit Court for the facts to be investigated. There, it was found that the order had been made bona fide. The applicants put in evidence a council memorandum entitled 'The Itinerant Problem'. However, nine councillors swore that they were concerned only with health matters, and their evidence was accepted. Yet one feels that the applicants had at least won a moral victory.

The situation rather recalls the cartoon with which the humorous magazine *Punch* (in March 1912) jeered the findings of the British parliamentary inquiry into the Marconi scandal in which it was alleged that government ministers had profited by the purchase of shares in a company to which government contracts had been awarded. A Liberal majority on the select committee exonerated the ministers. The findings were the subject of a cartoon in *Punch* that depicted Lloyd George and Rufus Isaacs leaving the committee room, with the chairman saying: 'You leave the Inquiry, boys, without a stain on your character, apart from the whitewash!'

CONCLUDING COMMENT

One has to see these cases – *O'Mahony* was decided in 1941, even earlier than *McGeough* (1956) or *McDonagh* (1966) – with the eye of the time. Irish public law has come so far so fast that it is necessary to remind oneself of the extent to which Gerald was making bricks with precious little straw. We have cited earlier the state of academic knowledge in Professor Kelly's time. But in the early 1940s, lectures on administrative law at Irish universities and books on the subject were even further in the future.[7] In the UK, this was a period that S.A. de Smith was to characterise as 'the twilight of Judicial Review'. The quotation is from the preface to de Smith's trailblazing work, which discerned and articulated the principles of judicial review for the common-law world and which did not come out until 1959.[8] To draw a medical analogy, Gerald's achievement was the equivalent of a doctor being able to prescribe penicillin (not discovered until the late 1920s or commonly available until the late 1940s) for his patients during the First World War.

It is true that, as far back as the late nineteenth century, the constitutional historian, F.W. Maitland, had written:

> If you take up a modern volume of the reports of the Queen's Bench Division, you will find that half of the cases reported have to do with administrative law; I mean such matters as local rating, the powers of local boards, the granting of licences for various trades and professions, the Public Health Acts, the Education Acts, and so forth.[9]

But what Maitland had in mind as 'administrative law' were the reams of collectivist statutes that were the legal form taken by the Industrial Revolution and the welfare state. On the other side of the balance was the need to secure protection and, where necessary, redress for the individual against government maladministration. This was surprisingly underdeveloped until the late 1960s: as we can see from the Kelly quotations, in Ireland – as indeed in Britain – lawyers were surprisingly late to address the problem of how the vast reservoir of state power could be reconciled with individual rights. This is truest of course where these collectivist statutes impacted mainly on the poor rather than the rich. Contrast the differing treatment of social welfare and taxation legislation. In fact, the great theme of the past two generations in terms of legal development has been how to ensure that these administrative powers may be exercised comprehensively by politicians and officials so as to benefit the community, but also in a reasonable and civilised fashion so as to respect individual rights. In this feat of reconciliation, *O'Mahony* takes rank as a precedent that helped to develop an informed and fair balance between the needs of the community and the individual.

Here, we ought to widen the focus of the discussion in order to reflect – and respect – the fact that Gerald, as well as being a solicitor, was a city councillor for eighteen years. For there are many and diverse ways of remedying injustice arising from governmental maladministration. The High Court, administering the bloc of law – judicial review of administrative action of which we have reviewed three leading cases – is one way. But the High Court is an expensive and inaccessible place, and relatively few instances of maladministration surface as court cases. There are many other ways of calling public servants to account and quelling the insolence of office. For instance, traditionally, public representatives have seen it as their principal duty to use their moral authority, behind the scenes, to remedy grievances of individual constituents against governmental services, a fact reflected in Basil Chubb's golden study, 'Going about persecuting civil servants: the role of the Irish parliamentary Rrepresentative'.[10] Next, there are statutory tribunals, such as An Bord Pleanála or the Appeal Commissioners of Tax, to oversee government administration. Again, for the past twenty years we have had one of the most active ombudsmen in the world. Finally, one should note the

Administrative Procedure Bill, which has been incubating in the Department of Finance for the past eight years. It is anticipated that this will set out a number of principles of good administration to which public bodies will be expected to adhere. These will include: the fixing of minimum response times; the provision of adequate information; and the establishment of appeal or other grievance mechanisms. This bill is based on the sound principle of remedying grievances at as low a level as possible. It will stipulate a person in each department or agency to whom a complaint may be made if any of these principles is violated.

Appraising these diverse ways of remedying public administration remains a challenge for research, research that would undoubtedly do the state some service, whether it would know it or not. It would involve: assessing the relative strengths and weaknesses of these various methods; how often and how significantly each is used; and the implications they carry for openness and accountability (we refuse to add on 'transparency' to make up 'OAT' because we cannot see the difference between openness and transparency). This would be empirical research of a high order that would engage the attention of someone qualified in public administration and public law. It will not be essayed here, save to offer the striking figures that the number of judicial-review applications and ombudsman complaints in this jurisdiction are five times and four times, respectively, those in the UK (allowing for the difference in populations).[11]

Here, we seek to make only the simple point that in the field of casework, given the diversity of complaints (some of them justified, some not) that may be thrown up by the range of administrative functions, whether at local or central level, and the wide diversity of remedies, it is good to have public representatives who can comprehend the complexities of this field of casework. Democracy is only as strong as the quality of the elected representatives, and it is important (though an ideal that is not always achieved) to have politicians who understand the above complexities and subtleties. Plainly, there is no need for all politicians to be lawyers, but it is useful to have a critical mass of people who can comprehend how the law affects their constituents, master the intricacies of drafting, and follow the existing legal and constitutional framework within which new policy must sit.

Historically, in other jurisdictions, the general figure is given that twenty per cent of public representatives have been lawyers. To a curious degree this has not been the case in Ireland. For instance, in the twenty-ninth Dáil (2002–07), out of 168 members, only nine gave their occupations as solicitors, five as barristers. And out of the 560-odd members of the county and city councils elected in 1999, there were only fourteen solicitors and five barristers.[12] It is, of course, easy to see why successful lawyers do not wish to embark on a parallel career in politics: the demands on time and ravages on privacy are brutal; going ten rounds with the rough beast of the electorate is traumatic (*pox populi; pox Dei*, as one defeated candidate remarked informally); the damage to legal practice may be severe. One can think of a hundred reasons why not. All credit, therefore, to the select group who give their experience and expertise to this form of public service, among the chief of whom was Gerald. One might add a reference here to John J. Horgan, also a Cork solicitor and puzzler over municipal problems, the only begetter of the city and county management system, which was first brought into law as the Cork City Management Act 1929. A fascinating book awaits its author, comparing the personality and work of John J.

Horgan and Gerald. But Mr Horgan did not put himself before the electorate.

The lawyer-politician has, on the whole, been a distinguished breed, aware of the potential of, and the need for limitations on, power within the polity. Another relevant observation is Bacon's wise saying that 'reading makes a man full; writing makes a man exact; and speaking makes a man ready'. Each of these generalisations is illustrated and illuminated by the achievements of Gerald Goldberg: scholar, lawyer, politician.

Gerald Yael Goldberg[1]

DAMIEN O'MAHONY
WITH DERMOT KEOGH

The oral evidence of his son – the distinguished Cork solicitor, Gerald – and the unpublished memoir of his daughter Fanny, – mother of the novelist David Marcus – supplement the oral history of the early life of Louis Goldberg in Ireland, and provide a vivid portrait of the early years of the Jewish community in Limerick.

Louis Goldberg was, according to Gerald, a native of a Lithuanian village, Akmijan, in modern-day Lithuania. When he left his homeland in the latter part of the nineteenth century to find refuge abroad, his travels took him by boat from Riga in Latvia to Cobh and the port of Cork. He left for both political and economic reasons. He was leaving behind a country where there was a high level of discrimination against Jews, and they were precluded from being able to make a living in the professions. The road out of Russia offered both challenges and dangers, but there was also the prospect of a normal life and of being able to make a living and raise a family in relative safety and security.

The assassination of Tsar Alexander II on 13 March 1881 in St Petersburg intensified the plight of the Jews in Russia. The attack was carried out by a group of revolutionaries, but in the popular mind the tsar's death was seen to have been at the hands of Jews. What followed was a period of widespread anti-Semitism, culminating in attacks on Jewish villages. In a climate of intimidation and persecution, many left for western Europe and the US. Their arrival in Britain and Ireland was a landmark in the history of these islands.

According to family memory and folklore, Louis Goldberg was among that wave of Russian Jews who fled. According to Gerald, he had been conscripted into the Russian army at the age of fourteen. But before he could serve as a soldier, he fled his home in Akmijan. Economic factors, however, cannot be divorced in the case of Louis Goldberg from the prospect of being conscripted into the army of the tsar, which was noted for a strong anti-Semitism. Louis made the hazardous journey to Riga, where the authorities turned back a number of other boys in his group seeking to emigrate to the US. Possibly because of his fair colouring, he was allowed to proceed, and he found passage on a timber ship sailing to Ireland. This was supposed to be the first leg of his journey to the US. He had never seen a map before coming to Ireland; therefore, he did not know how far Ireland was from the US. The year was 1882.

Put ashore at Cobh, he had the good fortune to be met by another Lithuanian Jew, Isaac Marcus, who regularly went to the docks to offer help to newly arrived co-religionists. He was taken to the home of the Sandlers, who had also come to Ireland from Akmijan. There, Goldberg first met Rachel, who was to become his wife in 1891; she had arrived in Cork with her family from Lithuania in 1875 as a one-year-old child. The Sandlers kindly allowed him to rest for a few days in their home, where he became familiar with members of the small but growing Jewish community in Cork, his lifelong friend Zalman Clein among them.

Louis set out on foot for Dublin – a distance of 158 miles – within weeks of his arrival, according to his son Gerald. There, he met a co-religionist named Jackson, who loaned him ten shillings with which he purchased a pedlar's licence and a small stock of holy pictures of Catholic saints and popes. He returned to Cork on foot, selling his merchandise on the way. Thus, Louis began his life on the roads of southern Ireland, travelling around Limerick, Clare, Kerry and Cork with his wares on his back. He moved to Limerick in 1883, where a small Jewish community had congregated and where he had family and friends from Akmijan. He was taken in by his relatives, the Greenfields. The Weinronks, who had arrived from Akmijan in the 1870s, were his cousins. The two families remained very close during their Limerick sojourn. Goldberg was most probably related on his father's side to the Barrons, another Jewish family in Limerick. Louis Goldberg continued in the same line of work, travelling around the city and countryside.

According to the census returns, there was one Jew living in Limerick in 1861, two in 1871 and four in 1881. The number rose from thirty-five in 1888 to ninety in 1892 and 130 in 1896. About twenty-five families of Lithuanian Jews had settled in Limerick by 1900, mainly in the poor section around Edward Street.

Louis' daughter Fanny, born in 1893, recalled in her memoirs the harsh life of her father. She remembered seeing the pedlars walking through the streets of Limerick laden with their goods strapped on their shoulders and, sometimes, with picture frames hanging on their arms: 'Rain and cold didn't cry halt. They had their families to keep,' she stated. They were often known to their customers as 'tally men'. Working on the weekly-payments system, the debt was marked down in a book and the 'tally' added up. With their broken English, the word 'weekly' became 'vickla'. In certain Jewish communities, that was the only word used to describe their business as 'tally men'. As they went about their work, Fanny also recalled that children in the streets of Limerick used to run after the 'tally men', with their backs bent under the weight of their packs, shouting 'a pitchie [picture] man, a tally man, a Jew, Jew, Jew'. 'I wonder often how they lived,' she reminisced. The 'weeklies' also worked on foot in the countryside, returning to the cities at the weekend in time for the Sabbath.

His son Gerald, born in Cork in 1912, recalled that his father had been shown great kindness and hospitality by countrywomen in Co. Clare. On one occasion, Louis, who was a strict Orthodox Jew, was invited into a cottage and offered a glass of milk by the woman of the house. He politely refused but offered instead to milk the cow. Befriended by the family, he was allowed to sleep in the house, where – on other visits – he learned to sing lullabies in Irish that he later sang to his own children. It was, however, more usual for Louis to sleep in an outhouse while on the road. His was the common lot of the Jewish pedlar – a frequent sight in turn-of-the-century Ireland.

When prosperous enough in the mid-1880s, Louis rented a house in Mount Pleasant Avenue, off Coloney Street, in Limerick. He brought his mother over from Russia; Buba (grandmother)

Elka became a very strong force in his life, in that of his future family and in the life of the community. She became a much-loved member of the Limerick community, and helped to maintain the Lithuanian Jewish-family traditions. Louis, who used to travel to Cork as often as possible to buy stock for his business, frequently visited the home of the Sandlers at 13 Elizabeth Terrace, Cork. One day he saw a beautiful young women scrubbing the wooden kitchen floor; it was Rachel, the girl he had first seen as an eight-year-old child when he had landed in Ireland in 1882. He was introduced to her by her mother. He was so impressed that he immediately visited his old friend from Akmijan, Zalman Clein, and told him that he wanted to marry the girl. He asked Clein to make the match. She was seventeen and he was twenty-four. Never allowed to 'walk out' together, the couple were married on 18 September 1891 at the *shul*, or synagogue, in 24 South Terrace, Cork. They went to live in Limerick at 50 Colooney Street, next door to Coll's public house. Louis ran a small grocery shop from the house and continued to travel as a pedlar.

Later in the decade, the family moved to 47 Henry Street, where Louis had a small drapery store. While the business did not provide the family with a luxurious standard of living, Buba Elka was a strong woman known for her wonderful baking and her capacity to improvise. When, for example, kosher wine was not to be found in Limerick, she made it for special religious festivals. Rachel's mother also travelled from Cork, sometimes with her younger children, to help look after the household when her daughter had a child. By 1901 she had two daughters, Fanny and Molly (b. 1896), and one son, Henry (b. 1899). She had another boy in 1904. In all, Rachel had thirteen children who lived. Rachel's brother, Joseph Sandler, also lived with the family for a time, as did Louis' youngest brother, Solomon, or Sol – later a significant figure in the Zionist movement. Thanks to Louis' financial help, his two other brothers, Bernard and Samuel, had also come to live in Limerick by the turn of the century. Samuel lived at 15 Emmet Place with his wife Rachel and their two sons and two daughters; Bernard lived at 9 Coloooney Street with his wife Sima and their three daughters and three sons. Their cousins, the Weinronks, lived nearby. According to the 1901 census, Bernard Weinronk lived at 27 Bowman Street with his wife Sarah and daughter Jennette. David Weinronk lived at 46 Coloooney Street with his wife Sophia, daughter Hanna, aged twenty, and son Simon, aged eighteen.

Fanny (Frances Rebecca) recalled from her childhood that, for her, 'there has never been anything so beautiful and so gracious as the Sabbaths we had in the kitchen in Coloooney Street'. What follows is not a description of 'gracious living' but rather of the effort made by a family of committed Jews to observe the Sabbath with due solemnity:

> Buba always did the cooking and serving, my mother looking after us children, and helping my father in the shop. The table was always beautifully laid with a white tablecloth, sometimes lace trimmed, with the candles lighting in the shining brass candlesticks. These candlesticks were brought over from Russia by Buba. (When Molly got married, uncle Sol, who had kept them after Buba died, gave them to her.) The cutlery cleaned and a cruet stand was in the centre of the table with the various condiments in the cut glass bottles. The stand was old Sheffield plate polished to the gleam of silver. Wine was in a cut glass decanter, a very lovely one as I remember it.

On Friday evenings, the shop was closed and the older members of the Goldberg family changed into their best clothes and went to *shul*. Rachel remained at home with the children: 'When father came home there was the washing of hands, and Kiddush [prayer]. His exquisite baritone voice made every Kiddush a memory.' There followed the blessing of bread. A piece was given to each person seated at the table. The special bread was baked twice a week and it was 'beautiful in taste and looks. No bread has ever been so beautiful as that bread baked by my Buba Elka.'

Louis Goldberg and his brothers learned to read and speak English quite quickly. All had been well educated in Lithuania. Sol, for example, had studied to be a rabbi but had been expelled from the school very early in his career for reading late at night a work that had been placed on the banned list. In her memoirs, Fanny records that they 'devoured newspapers and anything in print they could get hold of. How often I heard the names of Parnell, Kitty O'Shea, Michael Davitt and all the names of the famous Irish politicians of the day.' She recalls that her father was a staunch Parnellite all his life, and blamed the British for his downfall. He felt that they had engineered the whole affair with Mrs O'Shea right from the beginning because he 'was a thorn in their side'.

The family first set up in Limerick, where Gerald's father was a cantor in the synagogue. Anti-Semitism, however, reared its ugly head and, in an attack in Limerick in 1904, Louis Goldberg was beaten up and later boycotted. Ireland, at this time, had its own share of anti-Semitic prejudice. Writing in the *United Irishman*, Arthur Griffith, on the subject of Jews and the newspapers that supported them, had this to say: 'All Jews' rags represent nothing but the impotent ravings of a disreputable minority which is universally regarded as a community of thieves and traitors.'[2] Gerald's father moved to Cork city in 1904.

Louis Goldberg was an Orthodox Jew. Despite only Orthodox Hebrew text being permitted, he was familiar with the literature of other peoples. He read Dickens in English and Pushkin in Russian. In those days, the Jews of Lithuania, Poland and Russia had begun to publish Yiddish literature, and these papers often contained contributions from other cultures. Franz Kafka, for instance, was a member of the Yiddish Literature Society in Prague. Gerald describes his father as being rarely without a book in his hand. He was a little unpopular with other Jews for his refusal to live in the ghetto, the area around Albert Road in Cork city, which was known as Jewtown. Louis was a Talmudic scholar, and Gerald grew up in a household immersed in Jewish law. He remembers that only Yiddish was spoken in their home, and that their religion was in keeping with Lithuanian practice. His father worked during the Great War as a jam-jar supplier to Crosse & Blackwell's factory in Cork, when such jars could not be imported from abroad. Louis Goldberg spoke six languages, according to Gerald, and never kept a gramophone or wireless in his house. Everything he did reflected his Jewishness. His father loved to sing, and his family would join in with him as he sang on the night before the Sabbath.

> My father had a wonderful voice. And my mother, who was a very timid and frightened woman after the events in Limerick, would wear all white and there'd be a white tablecloth on the table. We all sang, all thirteen of us. And we spoke Yiddish at home; it's a great language to tell jokes in.

Gerald Goldberg was the eleventh child in a family of twelve, and was born in Cork city on 12 April 1912. Like his forebears, Gerald described himself as a member of the tribe of Cohanim and, as such, had certain religious duties. That did not stop young Goldberg mixing with the children of Cork, whose playground was the city's streets. As a child, he knew the kindness and gentleness of prostitutes who played with the city children while waiting for the sailors off the boats on Cork's quays. These children went barefoot. Though the Goldberg family eked out a living, their children enjoyed the luxury of boots. However, Rachel Goldberg insisted that if her sons wanted to join the other children on the streets, they would have to remove their boots and socks 'as to wear them would have been an affront to the other children'. In pre-asphalt days, when streets were covered with cobblestones or just mud, children often played outside until late into the night. The children with whom Gerald played told him terrifying stories of banshees, and taught him how to play hurling and how to fight, though violence never appealed to him. He recalled watching local men play pitch and toss on Parnell Place, where he lived.

Growing up during a time of political upheaval, he felt it was 'natural to be a Republican':

Me and my friends we were all Republicans. We sang Republican songs which we used to learn off the posters stuck on walls by the IRA. But it wasn't all songs. The Black and Tans in Cork surrounded a house occupied by Republicans who tried to escape, were captured, had their noses cut off and their eyes gouged out before being killed.

He recalled seeing the bodies in the North Cathedral in Cork and, in his own words, he 'grew up a rowdy'. His father outwitted the Black and Tans by hanging a picture of the marriage of Prince Edward and Princess Alexandra in their home, thereby stopping the search party in their tracks during a raid. The picture drew a respectful salute and swift departure from the Black and Tans, the officer in charge happy in the knowledge that the Goldberg household was not a republican 'safe-house'. Louis Goldberg remembered, according to Gerald, that in Lithuania a similar plan had been hatched to save the family from the Cossacks.

One of Gerald's distinct early memories was of standing outside City Hall with the thought of one day being lord mayor, probably inspired by his strong connection with MacCurtain and MacSwiney, both of whom he had seen lying in state at City Hall. He recalled how, as a young boy, he attended the lying in state of Lord Mayor MacCurtain and was stunned to see that one of MacCurtain's fingers, which had been hit by a bullet, had turned black and that rosary beads draped his hands. The assassination of MacCurtain and the subsequent death on hunger strike of Lord Mayor Terence MacSwiney had a profound affect on him. Gerald's memories of this time were both vivid and emotive. He was moved greatly by the sacrifices made by these two exceptional men. He idolised MacSwiney and MacCurtain, and their example made him look upon the job of lord mayor as if it had a talismanic significance. As a gesture of respect, he commissioned portraits of the two martyred lords mayor of Cork, which he loaned to Cork City Council to hang in the lord mayor's room.

But the real hero of his youth was Michael Collins. In a published interview, he spoke admiringly of Collins:

Collins – I heard him speak four times. He was, oh, a

wonderful speaker. He had a marvellous voice. He would have been a Chaliapin if he sang. He was a broad man with a clear face and a big Clonakilty accent. I heard him speak in Cork and he stood at a rostrum. He suddenly brought his hand down on the rostrum with a thump! And the rostrum broke as if he had given it a karate chop. I have that voice in my head ever since and that crack in my heart.

Gerald recorded in another interview:

We mourned Kevin Barry and when the Black and Tans Crossley tenders came down the street – you could always hear them coming – we sang 'I'm Forever Blowing Bubbles' in memory of him. The British were supposed to have taunted him with that song as they hanged him.

He spoke of the shock and fear he and his brothers felt upstairs in 10 Parnell Place the night that Cork was burned. While the City Hall was on fire, the Goldbergs, and all the other families in Parnell Place, were evacuated. The following day was spent leaning against Danny Burns' property, watching all the ensuing activity.

The Goldberg boys had the broadest Cork accents imaginable. Arguing that they were completely out of control, their mother persuaded their father to send them to McAuley College, a Jewish boarding school in Sussex. Gerald described it as being 'a place full of upstarts', but he had looked forward to going there despite his republicanism: 'I had read the *Gem* and the *Magnet*, and I knew Billy Bunter and Harry Wharton. The idea of having a pillow fight in a boarding school appealed to me.' The Goldbergs only lasted a few years before being returned home. He recalled in a published interview:

> A German boy had asked to be excused from the Armistice Day events as he felt it would be unpatriotic of him to salute the British dead. The school authorities agreed and it made my brother and me think. We then went to see the Headmaster and also asked to be excused on the grounds that the British had murdered MacSwiney and assassinated our Lord Mayor, Thomas MacCurtain. Well, he went through the bloody roof. We got three lashes each with the cane for suggesting such a thing and as a result, my brother ran away.

When the news reached their father, he ordered them back to Cork and enrolled them in the Presentation Brothers College, which, Gerald said, 'was like a holiday camp compared to the other place'.

Gerald studied law at University College, Cork, graduating in 1934. The law was a natural profession for him to enter: 'I come from a Talmudic family. We were immersed in Jewish law. My father would quote: "Justice, Justice, shalt thou pursue."' But in UCC, a strongly Catholic institution, Gerald encountered some intolerance. Nevertheless, he added: 'One shouldn't live with bitter memories.' He served his apprenticeship with the firm of Barry C. Galvin and Son, and later enjoyed his own practice. By the outbreak of the Second World War, Gerald Goldberg had his own legal practice in Cork. This, however, did not prevent him enlisting as a volunteer in the Douglas Local Defence Force (LDF). He recalled in a published interview:

I think Dev did the right thing by imposing a media blackout during the war and ensuring that Ireland played no part … I enjoyed my time with the LDF and it was a great leveller among men – it didn't matter who you were, we were all in it together. We were very good at marching, but when it came to shooting I'm afraid I wasn't much use. When we were issued three pellets each to practise with I hit my friend's target three times but I couldn't hit my own.

Gerald had married Sheila Smith from Belfast in 1937, whom he met while on a scouting trip to Co. Down in 1935. They had already started a family when the Second World War broke out. They had to make provision for the safety of the children in the event of a German invasion. Gerald said that he contacted his immediate neighbours, and they agreed to give shelter and protection if both the Goldberg parents were taken up in a sweep of the Jews of Cork by Nazi occupiers and their 'quisling' followers. He had also secured the help of the family of the woman who worked with his own family to send the children to her home in the country where they would be reared until after the war. Both his housekeeper and neighbours agreed that the children would be sent to Goldberg relatives in the US after the ending of hostilities where they would be raised as Jews. His three sons, John, Theodore and David, survived the war in neutral Ireland. Today, Gerald's grandchildren and great-grandchildren are spread as far as Dublin, Britain, Philadelphia and Los Angeles.

Gerald became a prominent and much sought-after member of the legal profession. He was an outstanding solicitor, and developed a very large practice. Both Gerald and Sheila were strong supporters of the cultural life of the city. He was a patron of the arts and a collector of twentieth-century Irish painting. He also acquired over the years an outstanding library of Jewish history and legal works, and was a lover of Shakespeare and modern English literature.

Gerald also had a great interest in politics. He ran as an independent and was elected an alderman of Cork Corporation in 1967. He made history by being the first member of the Jewish faith to be elected First Citizen in 1977, winning by eighteen votes to ten on a Fianna Fáil nomination, having earlier relinquished his independent ticket. He recalled with great admiration the generosity of Councillor Dave Buckley, without whose support he would not have been elected and who he remembered with great affection. In his 28 June speech as newly elected lord mayor, Gerald addressed those present in Irish, Hebrew and English, stating that he was a Corkman born and bred, and proud of his city and people. During his time as lord mayor, he visited the US – in particular, Pennsylvania, where he says he spent hours copying William Penn's notes on Cork and reminding the Pennsylvanians that they owed a lot to Cork. When on his travels, he was often asked if the people of Cork were anti-Semites; his answer was always the same – he gave them top marks for tolerance!

Gerald praised highly many of the officials and fellow councillors he worked with over the years:

I had the privilege of working with some very dedicated men and women over the years who worked selflessly for the good of this city. The likes of John Birmingham, Pearse Wyse, and other very strong lord mayors such as Pat Kerrigan, Hugh Coveney and Seán Casey. When I became lord mayor it was a very humbling experience to be working in a position that had such other notable incumbents. We are fortunate in Cork to have produced so many outstanding leaders and continue to do so.

Sheila also played a large public role during her term as lady mayoress. She visited schools around the city many times and fulfilled an almost 'First Lady' persona.

When asked what figures stood out in his mind of that time, he immediately listed Dave Buckley, to whom he felt he owed so much, followed by Peter Barry, Hugh Coveney and Jim Corr, all of whom he felt worked endlessly for the City Council and the people of Cork. He recalled with great fondness Joe McHugh, whom he considered a wonderful city manager and with whom he worked extremely well. On one particular occasion, prior to his mayoralty, McHugh had arranged for the gardaí to be present when a particularly contentious issue appeared on the agenda, knowing that a public mêlée would ensue. Goldberg recalled how quickly the gardaí entered the chamber, clearing it of a rather rowdy group who had interrupted the proceedings. He also related with humour how he was physically removed from his seat in the chamber and put over the barrier into the public gallery on another occasion.

He believed that there were wonderful men discharging their responsibilities as officials in those days, in particular city managers. During those decades, strong concentration, cooperation and understanding were needed, as well as the ability to satisfy every member of the council to ensure that the people of Cork would always receive the highest standard of treatment. Prospective lords mayor needed 'an ability to understand and to offer understanding to members of council and to spare no effort to achieve success of members' hopes'. He further believed that housing should be uppermost on any lord mayor's agenda.

Gerald Goldberg's time as an elected representative was a time of dynamic change in Cork. In 1976 Cork City Corporation embarked upon one of the most ambitious strategic planning exercises ever undertaken in the state's history. The Land Use and Transportation Study (LUTS) was an examination of the greater Cork area's development and transportation needs up to the new millennium – a period of twenty-five years. The delivery of the vision which had crystallised in the study's findings was a task of gargantuan proportions. Nevertheless, the council on which Gerald Goldberg served, as both an alderman and lord mayor, rose to the challenge. The success of the LUTS plan continues to be built upon today, with the recent adoption of LUTS' successor, the Cork Area Strategic Plan (CASP). CASP is a testament to the value of long-term strategic planning as a mechanism for the delivery of infrastructural and spatial-planning change. Gerald Goldberg played a pivotal role in the championing and shaping of the first such strategic plan introduced in the state.

After eighteen years of public service, his active role in politics came to an end in 1985. An increasing disenchantment with politics had slowly taken hold in this man of integrity. In an interview with the *Cork Examiner* that year, he said:

> I admired Charles Haughey but he has surrounded himself with rogues. I am very unhappy with politics in Ireland – there is no place in it for a person like me. It attracts the opportunists and the job-hunters. There are too many yahoos in the Dáil – it's the likes of ex-Gaelic footballers and the wives or sons of former TDs who get the votes. There's no place for intellect, for thought.

On his future with Fianna Fáil, Gerald said:

> I won't be a yes-man and I will support Dessie O'Malley. The
> day that Dessie O'Malley calls on me, I will go with him. If
> Haughey wants support from people like me, he must earn
> it. Fianna Fáil has become a dictatorship.

Speaking on the issue of press coverage of local politics, Gerald
had this to say:

> A lot of coverage is given to some councillors who'll get votes
> from bullies and blackguards. I refuse to play that kind of
> game with the press. I believe in reason and in telling the
> truth. Politics is not just about getting drainpipes fixed or
> getting houses through pull.

Gerald always spoke with great affection of his wife Sheila: of
her wonderful outlook on life, her many activities, and in particular the founding in 1986 of Abode, the organisation providing a
hostel, day-centre and independent-living programmes for people
with disabilities.

Sheila's brother Sydney was a painter, and through him Gerald
Goldberg came to develop an interest in the visual arts. He collected paintings and sculptures, among them works by Picasso,
Epstein, Le Brocquy, Chagall and Jack B. Yeats. Sheila was also a
great art lover. She befriended Elizabeth Friedlander, the Jewish
artist who came to live in Cork. Elizabeth bequeathed her port-
folios to Sheila Goldberg, and much of this archive is now lodged
in the Boole Library at UCC, another example of the Goldberg
contribution to the cultural life of Cork city.

Gerald and Sheila Goldberg will be remembered by many people for their patronage of the arts spanning several disciplines. Gerald was governor of the National Gallery and director of the Cork Opera House. Both he and his beloved Sheila were great supporters of live musical performances in Cork. He had a passion for books, and had a most comprehensive private library, a testament to his academic life and in particular his interest in Jewish history and fiction.

A man of words, he wrote several manuscripts of his recollections and those of his parents. Many will be familiar with the documentary written and presented by him, entitled *An Irishman, a Corkman and a Jew*, another opportunity taken to explore and record experiences for posterity. He was a great believer in setting things down for another era.

A non-drinker, he declared that he was always conscious of the job he had to do and how he should maintain the standards expected of him.

Gerard was conferred with the degree of Doctor of Laws in 1993, when the president of University College, Cork, Dr Michael Mortell, stated that 'Mr Goldberg contributed in large measure to the cultural life of Cork and the nation, and overcame hardship and prejudice to become one of Ireland's best-known and respected Irishmen, Corkmen and Jews.' Mr Goldberg's joy was summed up in his own words on the day: 'I was as happy as Larry to be made lord mayor and now this; I can ask no greater accolade from Cork.'

Gerald Goldberg travelled to Israel many times, but found it impossible to contemplate settling there: 'My thinking is Irish.' Solicitor, art lover, bibliophile, lord mayor, Jew, Irishman – but above all, a Corkonian! 'Cork is the only place that I've ever wanted to live. I love the people here, they're my kind of people. The Irish in general are a good bunch. We're honourable and courageous – in fact the only fault I find in them is that more people drink Guinness than Murphy's. Such a shame!'

The Dying Synagogue at South Terrace

THOMAS McCARTHY

Chocolate-coloured paint and the July sun
like a blow-torch peeling off
the last efforts of love:
more than time has abandoned this,
God's abandonment, God's synagogue,
that rose out of the ocean
one hundred years from here.
The peeling paint is an immigrant's
guide to America – lost on the shore
at Cobh, to be torn and scored
by a city of *luftmenshen*,
Catholics equally poor, equally driven.

To have been through everything,
to have suffered everything and left
a peeling door. *Yahweh* is everywhere,
wherever abandonment is needed –
a crow rising after a massacre,
wearing the grey uniform
of a bird of carrion, a badger
waiting for the bones of life
to crack before letting go:
wishing the tenth cantor to die,
the synagogue to become a damp wall,
the wailing mouths to fester.
Too small. To be a small people
aligned to nothing is to suffer blame
like a thief in the night. Some activist
throws a bomb for the suffering PLO:

the sky opens and rains a hail
like snowdrops. Flowers for memory,
petrol for the faraway.
To define one's land is to be a cuckoo
pushing others, bird-like, into a pit,
until at the end every national gesture
becomes painful, soiling the synagogue
door, like the charcoal corpses
at Mauthausen Station, 1944.

We who did nothing for you, who
remained aloof with the Catholic world
and would have cried *Jew*! like the others –
David forgive us –
we who didn't believe the newsreels,
preferring hatred of England to love of you,
we might shut our hypocrite mouths,
we want a West Bank but not a Stormont.
We have no right over your batons,
having made nothing for you but L. Bloom.

To sit here now in the rancid sunshine
of low tide is to interiorize
all of the unnoticed work of love –
exquisite children fall like jewels
from an exhausted colporteur's bag;
a mid-century daughter practises piano,
an *étude* to cancel terror; a nephew
dreams of the artistic life, another
shall practise law and become, in time,
the Catholic's tall Lord Mayor.
Where these jewels fall beside the peeling door
let us place the six lilies of memory;
the six wounds of David's peeling star. .

Notes on the Early History of Cork Jewry[1]

CORMAC Ó GRÁDA

Cork's Jewish community was never big. Fuelled by the immigration of Lithuanian Jews, the number in city and county combined rose from twenty-six in 1881 to 217 in 1891. It then fell back to 166 in 1901, but fortified by a high birth rate and an influx of some Limerick Jews (including Gerald Goldberg's father) in the wake of the boycott of 1904, it rose to 446 in 1911. It declined thereafter to 362 in 1926 and 226 in 1936 (*see* Table 1, page 85). Today, alas, the permanent Jewish presence in Cork is down to single figures and the community is no longer viable. The definitive history of this once-proud community remains to be written.[2]

One of the enduring myths about Cork Jewry – and Irish Jewry in general – is that they were 'accidental' communities.

Ronit Lentin describes her grandfather-in-law as one of a group from the village of Akhmian (today's Akmene in north-western Lithuania) who arrived in Cobh on a ship from Hamburg 'escaping forced conscription to the Czar's army'; they were 'instructed to disembark in the South of Ireland, told that this is America'. A US descendant of Dublin Litvaks (as Lithuanian Jews were known) believed that 'it was never my family's intention to settle in Ireland, but it was in fact an accidental landing point when they left Russia … a way station for some of the family, as most have made homes in other countries.' Another account, hilarious but less plausible, asserts that calls of 'Cork, Cork' were mistaken for 'New York', prompting 'befuddled, bedraggled, wandering Jews' to disembark in the city by the Lee. Yet another version has the Jews staying in Cork because, their ship being delayed there for repairs for several weeks, they ran out of kosher food.[3] Even Gerald Goldberg, himself the son of an immigrant, described the Litvaks' arrival in Cork as 'an accident'. They were landed in the port of Cork and duped by the claim that 'America is the next parish'.[4] Such claims are grist for the mill of collective memory, but they must be taken with a grain of salt as history. Good examples of what historian David Cesarani dubs the myth of accidental arrival, they are also a recurring feature of memoirs of Jewish emigration to Britain.[5] In reality, Cork would provide a decent living for several decades for the small number of Litvaks who settled there.

Cork Jewry was initially concentrated in a small area in the south-east of the city, south of the River Lee but not far from the city centre: it was never big enough to make the kind of communal leapfrog to middle-class suburbia that happened in Dublin and, to a lesser extent, Belfast. Several of the earliest arrivals from a cluster of *shtetls* in northwestern Lithuania settled in the cluster of recently constructed dwellings called Hibernian Buildings off the Albert Road *c*. 1880. The community had close links with those of Dublin and Limerick.[6] According to Larry Elyan, when his grandfather, Jacob Elyan, arrived in Cork in 1881 he expected to find a vibrant Jewish community, but there was not even an active synagogue in the city. 'They had a room in the house in which they were supposed to hold services ... but they never used it at all.' Instead of observing the Sabbath, his co-religionists went off to wherever there was a fair, selling 'all the Catholic things ... Catholic emblems ... Catholic pictures'. And they taught Jacob a few words of English and told him that he would have to do likewise himself. Jacob began a weekly-payment business, and 'barely made a living with it'. In time, according to Larry Elyan, he cajoled his co-religionists into observance, though they were very reluctant at first.[7] The story is surprising, given the ultra-orthodoxy and confessional factionalism for which Cork Judaism was noted in the 1880s and 1890s: perhaps the Jews who preceded Jacob Elyan were not Litvaks, but German pedlars.

At the outset, the community's focus was on Hibernian Buildings and nearby streets, within earshot of the Albert Road railway station and the city docks. Much of the streetscape today is as it was more than a century ago when the first Litvaks arrived.[8] Hibernian Buildings itself was a recently built triangular development of a hundred or so compact, yellow-brick, on-street dwellings. Each unit consisted of four rooms, including a bedroom up in the roof. Monarea Terrace nearby had small two-storey red-brick houses with a tiny garden space in front. One side of Eastville, another street containing many immigrant households, replicated Hibernian Buildings, while the opposite side contained

75

larger and more respectable two-storey units. All units had a privy in the back. The area still has an 1870–80s feel to it. Its housing stock represents the better kind of improved working-class housing favoured by Litvak immigrants in Dublin and Belfast. The smaller units were a terraced urban version of the rural-labourer's cottage, but the range of housing also encompassed the very lower fringes of the middle class. The synagogue was located on South Terrace, one of the main routes into the city from the south. Close to the city centre, it was within easy walking distance of the area known locally as 'Jewtown'.

Most of the elderly men would assemble in a square in front of Hibernian Buildings on Friday evenings and on Saturdays. The late Esther Hesselberg, who grew up as Esther Birkahn in Cork in the 1900s, remembered one Captain Levy, 'who must have been nearly a hundred years old', telling the youngsters tales of the hardships endured by the Jews under the reign of the Kaiser, 'stories our parents would never talk about'.[9]

In the early years, the fledgling community, divided between two parties led by the Jacksons and the Cleins, was notoriously fractious. Blows and insults were often traded, to the amusement of confused non-Jewish bystanders. The two factions buried their differences in 1895. Larry Elyan reminisced in 1972:

> Going through my grandfather's papers who died in 1928 I saw a letter addressed to him by the chief rabbi Nathan Adler … 'Dear Mr Elyan, I am very happy to hear that there is a *shalom* [written in Hebrew characters] in your community, but I regret that I am unable to [meet] your request to supply a *sefer torah* [again written in Hebrew], in view of what happened to the last one.' They hit each other over the head with it.[10]

Esther Hesselberg's brother, who ghost-wrote *shul* minutes for a fee of a shilling per meeting, was present at the historic meeting when the chief rabbi, Dr Adler, paid a pastoral visit to inaugurate the united *shul* in South Terrace:

> The celebration was graced by the presence of the Cork High Sheriff whom [Dr Adler] asked for an English speaker after the initial Yiddish orations. One noted member welcomed the 'extinguished' guest and hoped he would continue to work 'with his soldiers at the wheel', which caused the chairman to tell him to continue his oration in his best King's Yiddish and to keep his Litvak English for the *shul* meetings.

Cork Jews had a reputation for being very *frum* (pious). Nobody was allowed to carry even a handkerchief on Sabbath, and according to Esther Hesselberg

> … the only facility (now happily discontinued) was the provision of spittoons in the synagogue for bronchitic *baila batim*, and my brother used to tell me that those kosher hillybillys were 'dead eye dicks' and never missed their target. One proud boast of the Cork community in my early years was the export of its surplus *kihila* talent to Dublin in the persons of Arthur Newman, Jacob Elyan, Philip Sayers, and the Shillman family and many others who were destined to form a nucleus of Dublin's very successful effort.

The first of the Litvaks in Cork aroused keen curiosity from passers-by. Reassured that the new arrivals were ordinary mortals like themselves, some of the local people 'came back with gifts of food and some stools to sit on and small ornaments and an old mattress – and one woman even brought a framed picture of Jesus!'[11] Within a few years, however, it was a different story, when the perceived threat to 'honest labour' from a small number of Jewish cabinetmakers provoked an unanimous demand from the local trades council that the immigrants 'be hunted out of the city on the ground that they were ruining honest trade'. The council's proceedings were widely reported. In the course of a blatantly anti-Semitic outburst, one delegate added the resentful complaint that local Jews 'would not eat with or shake hands with a Christian'.[12] Cork's lord mayor, John O'Brien, hastened to remind readers of the London *Times* that the anti-Semitic remarks 'which proceeded solely from two individual members of a local trades council' did not reflect 'the feelings of the citizens of Cork'. At the same time, he noted that workmen anywhere, 'whether in the East End of London or the East End of Cork', would feel bitter at having 'as they think, the bread taken out of their mouths by the forced immigration of so many refugees'.[13] Calm was restored when the two Katz brothers, who employed the Jewish cabinetmakers, were arrested for frauds committed in England, but whether the cabinetmakers they employed remained on in Cork is not known.[14]

Mutual suspicions between native and newcomer were inevitable in the early years. Irish anti-Semitism has been much discussed (see, for instance, Keogh 1998; Lentin 2001). How Jewish attitudes towards non-Jews back in *der heim* coloured the Litvaks' initial feelings towards Corkonians also deserves consideration. A classic anthropological study of the East European *shtetl* describes its children as brought up 'to regard certain behaviour as characteristic of Jews, and its opposite as characteristic of Gentiles'. Gentile traits included 'emphasis on the body, blind instinct, sexual licence, and ruthless force'; the peasant 'gets drunk, he beats his wife, he sings a little song'.[15] According to Ewa Morawska, author of a study of Jewish immigrants in small-town America a century ago, 'in the eyes of the *shtetl*, the *goyim*-peasants represented everything a Jew, including members of the *proste* or uneducated strata of Jewish society, did not want to and should not be, and this value-laden distinction was inculcated in children from infancy'.[16] It would be surprising, indeed, if Cork's Litvaks did not bring their high self-esteem and sense of superiority with them.

In Cork, the immigrants lived cheek-by-jowl with locals from the start. Their numbers left them little choice.[17] Living so close to *goyim* for the first time, they will have encountered several who fitted the stereotype just described, but they will have found that most did not. Presumably, native Corkonians, too, shed their prejudices as they adapted to their Litvak neighbours. There are signs of communal harmony from relatively early on. In late 1894 the corporation, prodded by the mayor and the aldermen, granted the community 'a piece of ground in the best part of Cork' for the construction of a synagogue and school; and in the summer of 1896 the mayor invited the rabbi of the recently united community to the traditional 'throwing the dart' ceremony in the city's harbour.[18] Almost certainly, children helped to break the ice between neighbours. In time, Cork's Jewish quarter, like Dublin's Little Jerusalem, became a successful mini-experiment in multiculturalism.

Jessie Spiro was born in Cork in 1892. Her unpublished memoir, written in America six decades later, is mainly about Dublin, but she recalled the following two yarns from her early childhood in the southern capital:[19]

'Did you steal a chicken, mam?' was one of our popular stories. It happened when one young woman, shortly after her arrival in Cork from Lithuania, accompanied a group of young people to the Opera, and when walking home her escort was a young non-Jew. As they walked he chatted with her, and she smiled and nodded at all his wisecracks. The people immediately following, knowing that Ada was a greenhorn and could not speak a word of English, listened to the animated conversation they were apparently carrying on, and then one of the group said to him, 'You know she can't understand a word of what you are saying'. He said 'You are codding'. Then as the others all joined in, he turned to the young Jewish girl and said, 'Did you steal a chicken, mam?' and of course she smiled and nodded.

'Yes, yes, but no!' is another of our well-known stories. There was a grocery run by a Quaker named Barker, this was in Cork, and he was very kind and patient with the young matrons who came to purchase at his place. He was particularly nice to the foreigners, and always listened carefully to them, and tried to understand what they needed. One day one of the young women wanted some barley to put in her soup, and she went to Barker's. He asked her what she wanted, and she tried to tell him, but could not explain it to him, so he showed her around the shop. First pointing to the sugar, she said 'No', then he pointed to something else, she also said 'No.' Then he pointed to the dried peas and she said, 'Yes, yes, but no,' since one can put dried peas in soup. Then he pointed to the beans, and her reply was also 'Yes, yes, but no'. Then he pointed to the rice, and she got quite excited, saying 'Yes, yes, yes, but no,' since rice was almost like barley. Finally he pointed to the barley, and she said 'Yes, yes, yes.' He then told her it was called barley. It was in that way that many of the newcomers learned to speak English.

Cork may not have seemed an auspicious destination for immigrants in the 1880s or 1890s. The nineteenth century had been one of stagnation and de-industrialisation for the city. Population had peaked at 107,016 in 1831; it was only 75,345 in 1881, and 76,673 in 1891. However, as in Dublin and Belfast, the immigrants were specialists in an age-old avocation – peddling – which was well suited to a poor country. Other pedlars had long trudged the highways and byways of Ireland, but the immigrants brought something new. Irish pedlars had traditionally sold easily transportable items, such as ribbons, sewing needles, cheap jewellery, chapbooks, tea and tobacco for cash, or else they were paid partly in kind. The Litvaks sold dry goods (mainly clothes, home furnishings and holy pictures) on credit. The repayments were typically a shilling or two a week. Smaller sums would hardly have been worth collecting; bigger sums would have been beyond the reach of the poor. This was the instalment system by another name. The Litvaks thereby occupied a niche that provided a living in a poor city for the small number of immigrant household heads.

The numerical dominance of pedlars, travelling drapers, or so-called 'weekly men' among the newcomers is strongly hinted at in the warning of a Cork rabbi: 'Tomorrow is Monday, and the first day of *yomtov*. If any of you go collecting, I warn you that a curse will fall on you, and you will die.'[20] Census information corroborates: of the forty Jewish men living in Cork's Hibernian Buildings in 1901, thirty-two were described as pedlars in that year's census. The remainder included a butcher, a grocer, a rabbi, a house carpenter, a watchmaker, a huckster, and two teenage dentist's apprentices. In a database of married Jewish men in Cork's Jewish quarter in 1911, 'pedlar' and kindred occupations alone accounted for half the total (nineteen out of thirty-nine); in addition, there were three rabbis, two master craftsmen, two moneylenders, a picture framer, a photo enlarger, a glazier, a tailor, and nine dealers or shopkeepers.[21] Some of these Jewish householders kept boarders, typically single men in their twenties: nearly all were described as 'pedlar' or 'traveller draper' in the enumeration forms. The same goes for most householders' sons. In 1901 Harris Taylor of South Terrace, for example, was a master cabinetmaker; his seventeen-year-old son Lewis was a picture-framer, and his daughters Jane (20) a dressmaker and Becky (15) a tailoress. Clearly, the majority of Leeside Jews found work as self-employed petty traders: in this list of household heads in 1911 only the tailor, forty-year-old Maurice Taylor, is likely to have been a wage earner. A petition bearing the names and occupations of fifty-six Cork Jews in 1893 included twenty-one travellers, sixteen drapers and four dealers. There were only four tailors (*see* Appendix 1, page 89).

Peddling on the weekly system was an unpleasant and risky business, but it gave the first generation of immigrants a strong economic foothold. Their sons graduated to more respectable occupations, mainly as traders, businessmen and professional men. The community was resilient and rich in what economists and sociologists call 'social capital'. It spawned its own network of welfare and cultural organisations. People helped and trusted one another. Those starting off in business had access to start-up capital.

As in Dublin, educational achievements were much valued.

Cork's Jews – as early as 1891 – were the first to establish their own National school, in partnership with the Commissioners of National Education. It was located in two rooms attached to the little synagogue on South Terrace. I. Goldfoot, son of S.L. Goldfoot – dentist and leading light in the Cork Hebrew congregation and commandant of the Cork 'tent' of Chevovei Zion, a Zionist organisation – was one of the first Jewish pupils at the Cork Grammar School, and 'passed into the College of Surgeons' in late 1893. Somewhat later, two of Goldfoot's sons passed medical exams in Dublin and Edinburgh.[22]

Unlike their Dublin co-religionists, whose political sympathies were strongly pro-union in the 1890s and 1900s, Cork's Jews were rather nationalist in outlook from early on. Larry Elyan attended the Jewish National school, and remembered his 'first seeds of nationalism [being] sown there, in the songs we sang, they were always very Irish nationalist … interspersed with stories of Irish history, you know, in which were recounted all the injustices ever imposed on Ireland by Britain.'[23]

The Litvak immigrants brought their demography with them. In this respect, the demography of the Cork community a century ago is of special interest. What follows is based on an analysis of thirty-nine Jewish households (comprising about 200 Jews and some servants) and 148 non-Jewish households living in the same neighbourhood in the south of the city. Of the latter, ninety-four were Catholic, and six involved mixed Catholic–Protestant marriages. The most important features are described in Tables 2A–2E (pages 85–7). The Jewish couples had married earlier than non-Jews. In the case of brides, the gap was a striking four years (Table 2A, page 85). This accounts, at least in part, for the higher marital fertility of Jewish couples. Inevitably, any generalisations about Jewish fertility are based on a very small number of observations; even so, the Jewish advantage a century ago is clear (Table 2B, page 86). However, Jewish fertility would plummet in the following generation.

Another remarkable feature of Jewish demography almost everywhere a century ago was the much higher survival chances of Jewish infants and children. In Cork, too, Jews stood a better chance of surviving infancy and childhood than their non-Jewish neighbours. This may be seen from cross-tabulating the percentages surviving by duration of marriage (Table 2C, page 86). Thus, the higher survival chances of Jewish infants and children were not due to the lower fertility of their mothers.

In 1911 illiteracy was more prevalent in the Jewish community than in the host community (Table 2D, page 87). Thirty-one per cent of Jewish women in our database were illiterate, compared to four per cent of non-Jewish. Eighty-five per cent of Jewish men could read and write, compared to ninety-seven per cent of non-Jewish men. Given the reputation of Jewish communities for learning and the onus on Jews to learn how to read the scriptures in Hebrew, these numbers may seem surprising, but, as others have pointed out, illiteracy was by no means unknown in the Lithuanian *shtetls* whence Ireland's immigrants sprung.[24]

As in Dublin a century ago, the average Jewish household in the Jewish quarter seems to have been somewhat better off than its non-Jewish counterpart. Thus, eight of the thirty-nine Jewish homes in my 1911 database could afford a domestic servant, compared to only fourteen of the 148 non-Jewish homes. The Jewish households with one or more servants included four drapers, a furniture dealer, a herring exporter (Solomon Birkahn, Esther Hesselberg's father), a jeweller and a metal merchant. The average Jewish household also had more space at its disposal than its non-Jewish neighbours. In Cork, the numbers were 5.54 rooms per household for Jews, and 4.49 rooms for others. The respective standard deviations, 2.12 and 2.62, are consistent with less with-in-group inequality in the Jewish community at this juncture – by this criterion at least (Table 2E, page 87). Still, there was a clearly defined socio-economic pecking order within the community. This is reflected in the order in which the petitioners in Appendix 1 (page 89) were listed. The petition, dated 1 October 1893, reflects the Zionist feelings of Cork Jewry. The first half-dozen listed were comfortably off; poorer pedlars and travellers follow. All names from A. Goldwater down were penned in the same hand. This may indicate the illiteracy of those concerned, or their absence as pedlars or travellers when the petition was drafted. Note, too, the near-absence of residents of Hibernian Buildings in the list of Cork traders in Harfield's *Commercial Directory*, also published in 1893 (*see* Appendix 2, page 91).

The seeds of Cork Jewry's decline are already visible in the data for 1911–36 in Table 1 (page 85). While the Jewish populations of Dublin and Belfast continued to increase, that of Cork city and county fell back by almost half. Was this because of Dublin's pull-ing power: its wider choice of schools, or the better employment and marriage prospects afforded by its more elaborate Jewish social network? As Table 3 (page 88) shows, all religious denomi-nations other than Catholic suffered severe losses in this period in Cork city and county – considerably more than in the Irish Free State as a whole. Most of the decline predated 1926; the War of Independence and the radical shift in Cork's cultural and political complexion that followed it were responsible. However, Cork's Jewish population suffered most in 1926–36, a decade when the

Jewish population in the state as a whole rose marginally. Barring a miracle, it is to be feared that the Cork Jewish community that Gerald Goldberg represented and cherished has passed away with him. Given its size, Cork Jewry was always vulnerable: eventually, a rapid decline in marital fertility and the desire to marry within the faith brought the little community to its knees.

TABLE 1
THE JEWISH & RUSSIAN-BORN POPULATIONS OF DUBLIN, BELFAST, CORK, IRELAND

Year	Dublin	Belfast	Cork	Ireland
1861	324		0	393
1871	189	11	6	285
1881	352	61	26	472
1891	1,057	205	217	1,779
1901	2,169	763	166	3,898
1911	2,965	1,139	446	5,148
1926	3,150	1,149	362	5,044
1936–37	3,372	1,284	226	5,221

Note: 'Dublin' and 'Cork' refer to city and county combined

TABLE 2A
AVERAGE AGE AT MARRIAGE
(standard deviations in brackets)

	Brides	Grooms
Jews	21.7 (3.4)	25.9 (4.8)
Others	25.5 (5.6)	28.7 (7.0)

TABLE 2B

AVERAGE NUMBER OF CHILDREN BY MARRIAGE DURATION

(number of observations in parentheses)

Duration	Jews	All Others
0–4	0.75 (4)	1.18 (33)
5–9	3.86 (7)	2.00 (23)
10–14	4.83 (6)	3.27 (15)
15–19	6.00 (4)	4.21 (24)
20–29	6.73 (10)	5.94 (31)

TABLE 2C

PERCENTAGE OF COUPLES WITH NO CHILDREN BORN BY MARRIAGE DURATION

(number of observations in parentheses)

Duration	Jews	All Others
0–9	0.18 (11)	0.30 (56)
10–19	0.00 (10)	0.26 (39)
20–29	0.10 (10)	0.13 (31)

TABLE 2D

PERCENTAGE OF CHILDREN
STILL ALIVE BY DURATION

Duration	Jews	All Others
0–4	100.0	92.3
5–9	85.2	91.3
10–19	86.8	78.0
20–29	84.6	77.7

TABLE 2E

LITERACY IN 1911

(percentages in parentheses)

	Jews		Catholics		All Others	
	M	F	M	F	M	F
Illiterate	5 (13)	12 (31)	3 (3)	5 (4)	0 (0)	0 (0)
Read only	1 (3)	2 (5)	1 (1)	6 (5)	(0)	0 (0)
R & W	33 (85)	25 (64)	113 (97)	106 (91)	31 (100)	31 (100)
Total	39 (100)	39 (100)	117 (100)	117 (100)	31 (100)	31 (100)

TABLE 3

POPULATION & RELIGION 1911–36

Year	Catholics	C. of I.	Presbyterians	Methodists	Jews
Co. Cork					
1911	356,269	29,568	1,950	2,690	446
1926	345,119 (-3.1)	16,893 (-42.9)	818 (-58.1)	1,615 (-40.0)	362 (-18.8)
1936	338,461 (-1.9)	14,459 (-14.4)	661 (-19.2)	1,351 (-16.3)	226 (-37.6)
Irish Free State					
1911	2,812,509	249,535	45,486	16,440	3,805
1926	2,751,269 (-2.2)	164,215 (-34.2)	32,429 (-28.7)	10,663 (-35.1)	3,686 (-3.1)
1936	2,773,920 (+0.1)	145,030 (-11.7)	28,067 (-13.5)	9,649 (-9.5)	3,749 (+1.7)

Note: the numbers in parentheses refer to decadal percentage changes.
Source: *Ireland. Census of Population 1926, vol. 3(I): Religion*, Dublin: Stationery Office.

APPENDIX 1
NAMES & ADDRESSES ON
CHEVOVEI ZION PETITION, 1893

Name	Occupation	Address
A.H. Goldfoot	dentist	Grand Parade
M.L. Cohen	agent	20 Rockboro Road
J. Myers	clergyman	7 Rockboro Road
J. Solomon	shopkeeper	38 Shandon Street
I. Jackson	merchant	11 Monarea Tce
A.M. Edelstein	picture/glass warehouse	30 Old George Street
N. Taylor	dealer	5 Marina Terrace
Nathan Jackson	draper	81 Hibernian Buildings
J.M. Goldwater	draper	41 Hibernian Buildings
Nathan Baker	draper	4 Eastville
M. Bookman	draper	73 Hibernian Buildings
Joseph Levy	traveller	63 Hibernian Buildings
Zalman Levy	traveller	90 Hibernian Buildings
Jacob Sayers	draper	80 Hibernian Buildings
Abraham Sayers	draper	80 Hibernian Buildings
Philip Sayers	draper	80 Hibernian Buildings
Samuel Levy	agent	83 Hibernian Buildings
I. Abramowitz	picture frame maker	39 Douglas Street
Henry Jackson	draper	44 Hibernian Buildings
Lewis Bookman	dealer	13 Eastville
Abraham Horowitz	draper	80 Hibernian Buildings
A. Goldwater	tailor	Victoria Ville
Jacob Goldwater	tailor	Victoria Ville
Jona Goldwater	tailor	13 Old George Street
S. Levinson	tailor	21 Marina Terrace
Michael Lovish	traveller	4 Eastville
L. Clein	draper	2 Elizabeth Terrace
E.L. Jackson	shopkeeper	10 Marina Terrace
D. Bremson	draper	4 Eastville
H. Clein	traveller	30 Hibernian Buildings
I. Jackson	dealer	12 Eastville
S. Criger	traveller	9 Elizabeth Terrace
I. Friedman	shopkeeper	34 Hibernian Buildings
I. Jalkin	draper	6 Elizabeth Terrace

continued over

Z. Haddess?	traveller	11 Eastville
L. Glasser	dealer	2 Marina Terrace
I. Jackson	dealer	88 Hibernian Buildings
N. Baker	traveller	4 East Ville
I. Broidie	draper	83 Shandon Street
J. Lazarus	traveller	1 Monarea Terrace
S. Leibesman	traveller	1 Monarea Terrace
B. Davis	draper	93 Hibernian Buildings
Joseph Levin	traveller	6 Hibernian Buildings
Henry Jackson	traveller	44 Hibernian Buildings
S. Spiro	jeweller	10 Bridge Street
Lewis Levin	draper	8 Eastville
Lewis Levin	traveller	5 Marina Villa
A. Sless	traveller	4 East Ville
B. Joseph Heart	shoemaker	79 Hibernian Buildings
A. Taylor	draper	5 Marina Terrace
I. Rituffe?	traveller	5 Marina Terrace
M. Davis	traveller	84 Hibernian Buildings
L. Herzog	traveller	8 Monarea Terrace
I. Newman	traveller	92 Hibernian Buildings
L. Goldberg	traveller	32 Hibernian Buildings
S. Couffman	traveller	57 Hibernian Buildings
S. Levy	traveller	63 Hibernian Buildings

Source: Irish Jewish Museum, Box 5 (request to establish a branch of Chevovei Zion in Cork, 1 October 1893).

APPENDIX 2
TRADERS INCLUDED
IN HARFIELD'S DIRECTORY

Name	Business	Address	Since
L.S. Clein	wholesale draper/furnisher/boot dealer	4 Monarea Tce	1882
Meyer Elyan	general draper and jeweller	9 Monarea Tce	1881
G. Sayers	general dealer	8 Monarea Tce	1883
S. Spiro	jeweller	Bridge St	
E.L. Jackson	picture frame manufacturer/gen. draper	93 Douglas St	1883
L.S. Clein	drapers/outfitters/silk & boot merchants	49 Gt. George's St	
Hy. Jackson	draper/general dealer	44 Hibernian Bldgs	1885
Sol. Clein	wholesale and retail draper/furnisher	9 Marina Tce	1882
Lewis Glasser	wholesale and retail draper/furnisher	2 Marina Tce	1883
W. Jackson	wholesale and retail draper/dealer	11 Marina Tce	1880
Aaron Levin	draper/general dealer	16 Marina Tce	1885
N. Sayers	complete house furnisher	10–11 N. Main St	
A.M. Edelstein	picture frame manufacturer	30 Old George's St	
Rev. J.E. Myers	minister/sec. Cork Hebrew Congregation	Rockboro' Road	
Prof. Hartog	Cork University		
I. Abrahamson	draper/general dealer	7 Elizabeth Tce	
D. Bremsen	draper/general dealer	4 Eastville	1884
L. Clein	wholesale and retail draper/general agent	2 Montenotte View	1882
S. Goldberg	draper/general dealer	8 Eastville	
I. Jackson	draper/general dealer	12 Eastville	1884
J. Jalkinowitz	draper/general dealer	6 Elizabeth Tce	
Sol. Kriger	wholesale and retail draper/dealer	9 Elizabeth Tce	
I. Rosenthal	draper/general dealer	6 Eastville	

Source: Harfield, *Commercial Directory of the Jews of Great Britain.*

Irish and Jewish Roots

JULIA NEUBERGER

This essay comprises part of the R.I. Best Lecture that I delivered at the National Library of Ireland in 1996. I make it my contribution to the *festschrift* for Gerald Goldberg because it ties together (though in a very amateur and minor way) two great themes of Gerald's life: his Irish roots and his Jewish roots. It is an attempt to link themes in ancient texts, and to question whether they are universal or simply parallels between Irish and Hebrew/Jewish literature. The answer is that there is an element of universality about many early stories and legends, but there is a theme here that reappears time and again in the two very different literatures.

When I was asked to give the lecture, I groaned at my lack of Irish knowledge, for a love of Ireland and things Irish is not the same as knowledge. My studies for the lecture made me certain that I would now have to learn Irish, for there is so much more to read to which I could not possibly have access. And so I apologise for my lack of knowledge of things Irish beyond my affection for them, and my somewhat random reading. I was educated in England, read Joyce and Yeats but not Synge at school (despite doing A-level English), and have filled in some of the holes in a haphazard way ever since, supplemented with a great burst of modern Irish fiction when judging the Booker Prize, much of it wonderful.

But I thought it might be helpful to look at something I do know a bit about, which is the question of being Jewish, and compare some of the identity questions and themes with some of what I have gleaned from the Irish literary tradition. For deep in my gut, there is a sense of some extraordinary, but little recognised, similarities in the way that the language was rediscovered in both cultures (a form of national identity, of course), in the way the longing for land is expressed, and in the use of ancient stories (pre-Christian in Ireland, this deeply Christian country, pre-Jewish, pre-biblical in Jewish writing). If I can at least draw some threads together and look at how those issues are reflected in our different literary traditions, that may perhaps shed clues others may think worth exploring in a more scholarly way.

Let me at once say that I shall not be examining the portrayal of Jews in Irish literature. As far as Joyce is concerned, the theme has been done to death, in my view. I am certainly no expert, and there are many who have made their reputations as literary scholars looking at just that issue. My offering is more an examination of similar themes, an exploration that is just at the stage of scrabbling at the opening to the burrow, no further.

I would like to start with Navan Fort, once Eamhain Macha,

the seat of kings and the earliest capital of Ulster. This is where Conor (figure of early Irish stories) ruled; this is the home of kings and legendary heroes of the *Táin Bó Cuailnge*, 'The Cattle Raid of Cooley'. The legends associated with Eamhain Macha were first written down in the seventh century, and have some similarities with – and many who work there would like to claim a real resemblance to – Homer's Troy or, perhaps more accurately, ancient Camelot and the Arthurian legends. Eamhain Macha gets its name from the tale of Crunniuc, a worthy man who lived in the area, who saw a woman running through the hills and glens faster than any man or beast he had ever seen. Captivated by her, he took her as his love, but could not find out her name. She told him that it could only be spoken in another place. Years later, King Conor called on the people of Ulster to attend the royal games. The king's chariot, pulled by two magnificent horses, sped like the wind, but Crunniuc boasted that his wife could run even faster. Conor demanded to see this for himself, and if he did not, he would put Crunniuc to death. Crunniuc pleaded for the challenge not to take place because his wife was heavily pregnant, but the king was not in a mood to listen. So Crunniuc's wife ran the race and won. Conor asked for her name. She replied that her name was Macha, and that thereafter the place she lay would be called after her; hence (after she had given birth to twins) the name Eamhain Macha, the 'Twins of Macha'.

The twins symbolised, first, a blessing, giving Ulster's warriors strength and power, but the second twin was a curse, inflicting on Ulster's warriors a great fever at times of war, a fever like that of a woman heavy with child. The curse is at work in the *Táin*, where Queen Maeve of Connacht wants a bull to compare with her husband Aillil's 'Great White Bull'. The only one that will do is the pride of Ulster, the Brown Bull of Cooley, so the warrior queen vows to attack Ulster and steal the bull. Beset by the curse of Macha, the warriors of Ulster cannot protect their lands. Cúchulainn, the only one immune from the curse, has to defend Ulster single-handedly at the 'Gap of the North', the break in the ring of mountains protecting Ulster. He kills many of Maeve's warriors until the valley is full of bodies of Connacht men. Maeve tries everything, to no effect, until she sends Cúchulainn's boyhood friend, Ferdia, as her champion. Cúchulainn is desperately upset, for he hates to hurt the one he had loved like a brother as a child. But he fights a tremendous battle and drives his spear into Ferdia's chest, so lifting the curse of Macha. Warriors arrived to help Cúchulainn, pushing Maeve back into Connacht whilst Ulster's Brown Bull of Cooley charges with all its might and tears Ailill's 'Great White Bull' into pieces.

This is Cúchulainn in action taken from an eighth-century version though most used are twelfth century (in Lady Gregory's translation), but all date to a much earlier period:

He did a mad feat of turning his body around inside his skin. His feet and shins and knees turned backwards. His heels and calves and buttocks came round to the front. His calf sinews rose on the front of his shins and each round lump of them was the size of the balled fist of the warrior. His huge head-sinews stretched down to the nape of his neck, and every immense swelling of them was as big as the head of a month-old boy. One eye he sucked back into his head so that a wild crane could scarcely pluck it from the recess of his skull on to the middle of his cheek ...

This is literally magic, and all pitted against Maeve, whose husband argues that she is better off with him than she was before he married her. She tells him that she came into the marriage being queen, while he only had two brothers who were kings and was not one himself, and that she had plenty of cattle and warriors and a great genealogy. And then, according to the *Táin*, she admits that she had 'a strange bride-gift such as no woman before had asked of the men of Ireland, that is a man without meanness, jealousy, or fear'. Aillil relaxes – a compliment at last in what seems like a bedroom tiff. But Maeve continues that she had brought with her into the marriage …

> … the breadth of your face in red-gold, the weight of your
> left arm in bronze. So, whoever imposes shame or annoyance
> or trouble on you, you have no claim for compensation or
> honour price other than what comes to me – for you are a
> man dependent on a woman.

He argues that he had only decided to marry Maeve and thus become a king himself 'because I heard of no province in Ireland ruled by a woman save this province alone'. It then emerges that the bull claimed by Aillil is in fact Maeve's, but it has attached itself to Aillil, 'thinking it unworthy to be classed as "women's property"'.

The rest of the story is well known, but there are two points I want to make, to relate it to Hebrew and Jewish literature. The first, and the more minor point, is about the role of Aillil and the question of whether some scholars are right to argue that the story of Maeve and Aillil is a representation of a shift from matriarchy to political patriarchy, on the basis of the argument that matriarchy precedes patriarchy in all cultures. The evidence is limited, but there is a story in the Hebrew Bible (what many people would call the Old Testament) where the same question may well be asked. Let me remind you of the story of Isaac's wife, Rebecca. (Genesis 34)

Abraham sends his servant to find a wife for Isaac. This already presupposes that Isaac is a weak man, an impression that does not diminish as one encounters him at other points in the book of Genesis. Abraham's servant arrives in Abraham's home territory of Haran – the nomadic merchant centre where flocks were traded and where Laban lives and others of Abraham's kinsmen – and vows to himself that the first woman who comes out and offers water for his animals and then sustenance for him and his man is the girl for his master's son. Rebecca comes out, offers water to the animals and to Eliezer. He in turn offers her gifts of fine gold and jewels, and they go to meet her family. But then comes the odd bit. Instead of going to see her father, as one might have expected in this patriarchal society (after all, we talk of the Three Patriarchs, Abraham, Isaac and Jacob), they go to Rebecca's mother and brother at the end of the negotiations. It is they who give their permission, and they with whom the negotiations on bride-price take place.

How strange. Where was Bethuel, Rebecca's father? Some argue that he had died, and that is why there is the request for her to stay behind for a few days (Genesis 34:55), to sit out the period of mourning. But the text does not say that, and one might have expected it to do so if that was indeed the case; it is full of births and deaths and the genealogical tables of the early Israelites, after all. Instead, scholars have taken the same view as they do with Maeve and Aillil: that this is the changeover from matriarchy to patriarchy, and that what we have here is the halfway stage of fratriarchy, where the brother and mother make the decisions – a structure known to the ancient Hurrians – a stage that eventually merged into patri-archy as we know it. In any case, the competition over wealth, and the curious discussion over who makes decisions and how, has some similarities with the Maeve story.

But that is merely a sideline. The more interesting compari-sons are not in the Hebrew Bible, but in the Midrash, a corpus of Jewish tales that used to be largely disregarded by scholars as 'merely legend'. The interesting stuff, the meat of Jewish scholarly debate, was always the law. We are a people of the law, more than a people of legends. Legends are romantic. Law is basic. Legends allow the imagination to fly away. Law is tangible, and exercisable. But I am being unfair. Yet the Midrash is more than a single corpus, collected in one place. It was the way people used to explain certain stories in the Hebrew Bible, and was often first taught to children. It is in fact a Jewish form of theology, much neglected and underrated. It dates from about the first to the tenth century CE, and some of it may actually predate the writing of the Hebrew Bible, though it does not appear in documents until later. Like the *Táin*, it may be very ancient indeed, and certainly some of the tales within it suggest very early origins.

The essence of the Midrash is the stuff of '*aggadah*', the telling of the tale, as opposed to the '*halachah*', the way in which you must go, 'the path', which is the legal material. But as it was not recognised in the nineteenth century, when serious scholarship began on Jewish texts, they are not considered theological. However, they ask ques-tions about why things happened as they did; they add in parts of stories that are not in the Hebrew Bible, but throw light on other aspects of life; they take a particular point and raise several parables to help explain the Divine will. They are not foolish stories at all, but until the end of the nineteenth century (at which time many Irish legends also came to be studied seriously) they were thought to be of little interest compared to the great problems, such as the dating of the Pentateuch and the reworking of the Jewish legal texts, and their translation into German, French and English.

One character that bears some comparison to Maeve is Lilith, first wife of Adam, precursor of Eve. Queen of the night, she is an angel, a demon, a fantastical creature, yet she is not just part of what some disparagingly call the 'folk-religion of the Jews' (which is what women's stories are often classed as). Her existence, her mission, if you like, is partly to torment women, but it is also to explain how the species survived, and how there is power out there that cannot be controlled by a patriarchy, or God.

The story is that the Divine resolution to bestow a companion on Adam met the wishes of man, who had been overcome by a feeling of isolation when the animals came to him in pairs to be named. To banish his loneliness, Lilith was first given to him as wife. Like him, she had been created out of the dust of the ground. But she remained with him only a short time because she insisted on enjoying full equality with her husband. She derived her rights from their identical origin. With the help of the ineffable name, which she pronounced, Lilith flew away from Adam and vanished in the air. Adam complained before God that the wife He had given him had deserted him, and God sent forth three angels to capture her. They found her in the Red Sea, and they sought to make her go back with the threat that, unless she went, she would lose a hundred of her demon children daily by death. But Lilith preferred this punishment to living with Adam. The Midrashic material continues:

> She takes her revenge by injuring babies – baby boys during
> the first night of their life, while baby girls are exposed to her

wicked designs until they are twenty days old. The only way to ward off the evil is to attach an amulet bearing the names of her three angel captors to the children, for such had been the agreement between them. (*Legends of the Jews*, I, 65–6)

There is no doubt that Eve was to be subservient, and even then women were destined to be a trouble, and the cause of sin. Of course, in earlier Jewish thinking, the idea of women as the source of sin was not present. One of the interesting things is that much of the Midrash represents thinking you can find in the early Church fathers, and in Christian thinking generally. People who have viewed Judaism as a religion that stopped developing at the end of the Old Testament read this material with amazement, for much of it has strong similarities with Christian ideas, and rabbinic thought has much in common with early Christianity precisely because those who were writing and thinking were actually the same people. So, though traditionally Judaism does not regard the story of Adam and Eve as the story of the Fall from Grace, a view that became of great importance in Christian Ireland and explains much of the attitudes to women in later Irish history, nevertheless, some of the same ideas about their proclivities to being 'gadabouts' or 'eavesdroppers' is still there:

When I was pregnant with my first child, my father gave me an amulet which he had found in Italy during the war, an amulet which names the angels who were Lilith's captors – Sansevai, Chutz Lilith, and Semangelaf – so that I should be safe in childbirth, protected from the evil eye. (In the last of the four corners of the amulet are Adam and Eve.) My father does not believe in the evil eye, or even in Lilith, but

GERALD GOLDBERG: A TRIBUTE

alongside this highly legalistic structure that outsiders see as our faith, there is another aspect that is mystical, sometimes almost magical.

In the end, Lilith could not bear to be subjected to Adam, not unlike perhaps Queen Maeve and her battle with Aillil. The story of Lilith serves as a comparison to that of Maeve and the *Táin*, of course, but it also helps to show how in Jewish literature there is the same difficulty of reconciling two traditions: the legalistic, 'Orthodox', one (though the word 'Orthodox' does not quite convey that sense); and the mystical, imaginative, sometimes didactic, explanatory, theological one, that uses ancient stories to make its point.

'Making *Aliya*': Irish Jews, the Irish State and Israel[1]

DERMOT KEOGH

By the waters of Babylon, there we sat down and wept when
we remembered Zion.

Psalm 137

From the time of the Babylonian exile in the sixth century BC,
before the common time, Mount Zion, one of the hills of
Jerusalem, came to symbolise for Jews their longing to return
to their homeland. Zionism, a term first used in the 1890s, was
adopted by Theodor Herzl as the name for his political movement, which sought the return of the Jews from exile.[2] Zionists
sought the establishment of a Jewish National Home in Palestine,

which became the central idea in Zionism. The 'in-gathering of the exiles' was the primary goal of what in the early twentieth century became a worldwide movement. The word '*aliya*' in the title of this essay is derived from the word in Hebrew for 'ascent', or 'going up'.[3]

Immigration to Palestine between 1880 and the Second World War has been divided into five phases, or *aliyot*. The first *aliya* is dated between 1882 and 1903, when an estimated 20–30,000 Jews emigrated from Russia and the east to Palestine. That was the period in which Ireland experienced its largest immigration of Jews from Lithuania, who were fleeing the Russian pogroms.[4] The second *aliya*, 1904–14, brought another 40,000 mainly Russian Jews to Palestine. During the same period, eastern European Jews continued to arrive in Ireland, but in much smaller numbers than had been the case in the last two decades of the nineteenth century. The third (1919–23) and fourth (1924–31) *aliyas* together brought over 120,000 Jews to Palestine, the fourth alone numbering nearly 90,000 Jews, coming mainly from Poland. The fifth *aliya* covered the years 1932 to 1938; during this, some 200,000 immigrants, mainly from central Europe, came to Palestine. During the Second World War, about 80,000 Jews succeeded in entering Palestine legally and illegally. The same process continued after the war: over 50,000 Jews succeeded in getting in, despite severe restrictions under the British mandate. After the declaration of the state of Israel in May 1948, the flow of Jewish immigrants grew dramatically. The new state allowed free immigration.[5]

This essay examines Irish–Jewish relations in the late 1940s and 1950s, and Irish emigration to Israel during the same period. Dr David Birkhahn, who left Cork in the 1950s to 'make *aliya*', describes his own experiences in the final section of this essay.

THE RISE AND FALL OF THE JEWISH
POPULATION IN IRELAND

Ireland has always had a relatively small Jewish population. Although there had been Jews in Ireland from the Middle Ages, the number remained quite small until the last decades of the nineteenth century, when pogroms in Russia forced tens of thousands of Jews to flee for their lives. The Jewish population of the twenty-six counties that were to become the Irish Free State in 1922 increased from 230 in 1871 to 394 in 1881; this population increased almost fourfold during the 1880s, to 1,506, and then doubled again in the 1890s, to 3,006. That figure rose to 3,805 in 1911, before reducing slightly to 3,686 in 1926. The Jewish community in the South increased to 3,749 in 1936, and grew again in the following decade, to stand at 3,907 in 1946, which was the highest number it ever achieved. Thereafter, it declined to 3,255 in 1961, to 2,633 in 1971, to 2,127 in 1981 and to 1,581 in 1991.[6] By 1997, the Jewish population in the Republic of Ireland was estimated to be about 1,200, almost all of whom lived in Dublin, and the strength of the Irish Jewish community continued to decline in number in the early twenty-first century.

In Northern Ireland, the Jewish population had grown from 282 in 1891 to 1,342 in 1911, when 1,139 lived in Belfast. The figure rose to 1,352 in 1926 and 1,472 in 1937.[7] It reached its highest point in 1951, with a population of 1,474, of whom 1,140 were resident in Belfast. There were 1,191 in 1961, 959 in 1971, 517 in 1981 and 410 in 1991, with most of the community over fifty years of age.[8]

Emigration to Israel was one of the main reasons for the decline in the Jewish population, North and South, in the second half of the twentieth century. It was not the most important

107

reason; the emigration of young Irish Jews to study abroad and to live in larger communities in Britain, Canada and the US was much more significant. However, many Irish Jews made *aliya* and went to Israel from the 1950s onwards. They followed others who had, since the 1920s, left to live in Palestine. This was done for both religious and political reasons. While the history of Zionism in Ireland has yet to be written, it is possible to sketch in broad outline the central significance of that movement throughout the twentieth century for many Irish Jews.

ZIONISM IN IRELAND

Russian immigrants to Ireland at the end of the nineteenth century founded the Hoveve Zion group. It met in Camden Street synagogue. They were the first supporters in Dublin of the Jewish National Fund. The first local branch was founded in 1901 by Jacob Elliman, a Lithuanian immigrant described as being a 'staunch supporter of traditional Judaism and an ardent Zionist'.[9] Simon Cornick was the first chairman, but he retired after a few months and was replaced by Elliman. The latter held that post until 1937, when he was named life president.[10] J.Z. Gilbert, in the *Encyclopedia of Zionism and Israel*, adds the following:

> In 1907 the Dublin branch of the Order of Ancient Maccabeans, the Mount Carmel Beacon, was founded. In the 1920s the Dublin Jewish Debating Society was formed. It became affiliated with the Federation of Zionist Youth of Great Britain and Ireland. Later, it became the Tel Hai Beacon, a junior branch of the Order of Ancient Maccabeans ... In 1941 the Dublin Younger Commission of the [Jewish National Fund] was organised. The Children's and Youth Aliya Group

was formed in 1946, and its Younger Committee in 1961. A Society of Friends of the Hebrew University of Jerusalem was established in 1948. The Joint Palestine Appeal was launched in Ireland in 1951.[11]

Esther Barron founded the Dublin Daughters of Zion in 1900. Rose Leventhal was chairperson of that group for over forty years, and was succeeded by Ethel Freedman. She held office for eleven years, and was replaced by Annie Glass. The latter held that position in 1966, a year in which there were six Zionist women's groups in Dublin, one in Cork and three in Belfast. A Regional Council of Women Zionists, with headquarters in Dublin, co-ordinated their activities. They were affiliated to the Women Zionists of Great Britain and Ireland and to the Women's International Zionist Organisation.[12] The autonomous Zionist Council of Ireland was represented independently at the Zionist Congress in 1951, but the Irish organisation continued to maintain links with the London-based Zionist Federation of Great Britain and Ireland.[13]

Much more research requires to be done to trace the emigration of Irish Jews to Palestine in the early decades of the twentieth century. The case of Max Nurock is hardly typical, but it is worth recalling here. The son of two Lithuanian immigrants, William and Rachel Nurock, he had a distinguished career in Trinity College, Dublin, where he was awarded a number of academic prizes. He served in the British army during the First World War. He spent most of his working life in Palestine, where he served as junior chief secretary to the high commissioner, Sir Herbert Samuel. Later, he served in the Israeli diplomatic service.[14] Chaim and Jacob Herzog, the sons of the chief rabbi of Ireland, Isaac

Herzog, went to complete their education in Palestine in the mid-1930s. Their father became the chief rabbi of Palestine in 1937. Chaim served as an officer in the army, and later went on to become president of Israel. His brother Jacob had a distinguished career in the Israeli diplomatic service. He was offered but turned down the position of chief rabbi of Great Britain and the Commonwealth.[15] The Nurocks and Herzogs are but two examples of Irish Jewish families who went to Palestine in the 1920s and 1930s. Further research will reveal other cases of Irish Jews who exchanged Ireland for a life in Palestine.

The Zionist activities of Irish Jews attracted the hostile attention of many polemical Irish Catholic writers in the 1930s. Prominent among these were two clergymen, the Holy Ghost priest, Denis Fahey, and the Jesuit, Edward Cahill, while hostile articles also appeared in Catholic journals such as *The Cross*, the *Catholic Bulletin* and the *Irish Rosary*. These attacks took the form of various accusations: that many Jews in Europe were involved in revolutionary left-wing politics; that Jews were part of a global conspiracy made up of Freemasons and communists; that Jews had a double and conflicting allegiance to the country in which they resided and to Israel. The Catholic polemicists were usually of the view that Jews would always choose the interests of Zionism over the national interests of the country in which they lived. In this climate of suspicion and fear in the 1930s in Ireland, it is not surprising that Jews who were active supporters of Zionism did not seek nationwide publicity for that cause.

Éamon de Valera came to power at the head of a Fianna Fáil government in 1932. He served as Taoiseach for sixteen years and lost office in early 1948, a few months before the foundation of Israel. In the intervening years, he took a strong personal interest in the future of Palestine. He was a friend of the chief rabbi, Isaac Herzog. As minister for external affairs throughout the period from 1932 to 1948, he was in a good position to follow developments in the Middle East. His regular attendance at the League of Nations in Geneva brought him further knowledge of the politics of the region. According to his party colleague, Robert Briscoe, he showed himself to be interested in Zionism. De Valera, who was to visit Israel with Briscoe when he was out of office in 1951, sent the secretary of the Department of External Affairs, Joseph Walshe, to Palestine in the 1930s to report first-hand on what was happening there.[16]

A split in the Zionist Organisation in 1935 constituted a potentially serious source of disunity for the Jewish community in Ireland (this remains to be determined by further research). The original Zionist movement covered a broad spectrum 'from the right-wing, religious-orientated Mizrahi through the General Zionists in the centre to the left-wing Zionist socialists'.[17] Each of those general groupings was in turn divided into other groupings. Irish Jews gave their allegiance overwhelmingly to the Zionist Organisation. But a small number, led by Robert Briscoe, supported the New Zionist Organisation (NZO). Its founder, Vladimir (Ze'en) Jabotinsky,[18] was accused by David Ben-Gurion, who became the first prime minister of Israel in 1948, of espousing the cause of extreme nationalism and of imitating fascist methods.[19] Jabotinsky, in opposition to other Zionist positions, favoured the mass migration of Jews to Palestine. He attempted to persuade the British government to 'evacuate' the masses of Polish Jews to Palestine where, in 1935, 24,300 of the 30,703 people who entered the country were from Poland.[20]

Jabotinsky further disagreed with the leaders of Zionism,

Chaim Weizmann and David Ben-Gurion, over the proposal to partition Palestine contained in a British Royal Commission report published in July 1937.[21] This was a proposal for which de Valera had no sympathy, and he made his opposition known at the League of Nations.[22] Within two years, however, the British – with an estimated forty per cent of its entire field force tied down in Palestine – reversed its policy on partition, and imposed a strict quota on the number of Jews allowed to enter the area.

An NZO delegation, led by A. Abrahems, was sent to Dublin on 6 December 1937. The visit lasted until 12 December. Hardly an impartial source, the London-based *Zion News* reported that they had found among the Jewish community in Dublin 'an eagerness to become acquainted with the problems of Partition' and the policies of the NZO. A number of members of the Zionist Organisation, according to the report, decided to secede and join the NZO. It was decided not to make that news public until a further visit took place in the near future.[23] The *Zion News* also wrote on page one of the same issue:

Ireland, in particular, must be regarded as of special importance to the future of the Movement. That country has been exposed to problems and experiences not dissimilar, in many ways, to those of the Jewish people; and that of the Zionist Movement. Its own nationalist Movement has been split from top to bottom on ideological and political grounds, remarkably like the differences within the Zionist movement ... Zionist roots struck in Ireland at the present time may, in the future, produce fruits which few can, at the present moment, foreshadow or even approximately estimate.

Jabotinsky visited Dublin in December 1938. Accompanied by Robert Briscoe, who was then a TD, he met de Valera and returned to see the Taoiseach again after he had paid a visit to the papal nuncio, Paschal Robinson. No official minutes for these meetings have been located, but according to Briscoe's memoirs, Jabotinsky was cross-examined by de Valera; they discussed the Jewish rights to Palestine, and Jabotinsky drew certain parallels with the Irish Famine and with the dispersal of the Irish after that great tragedy.[24] Jabotinsky also had a meeting with Joseph Walshe at the Department of External Affairs. Afterwards, Jabotinsky said: 'My immediate impression [on twice meeting de Valera] was of that broad-minded humanity, that chivalrous consideration for a neighbour's sorrows and ideals, and that innate simple courtesy one almost instinctively associated with the very atmosphere of Éire.'[25] During the course of the visit, he established a Dublin committee of the NZO.[26] The presence of a branch of the NZO in Dublin did not add to Robert Briscoe's popularity among the majority of his co-religionists. Irish-army intelligence during the war years reported on Briscoe's Zionist activities; he was believed to be a member of the supreme body of the NZO.[27] Shortly before the war, Briscoe had gone on missions for that organisation to South Africa and to Poland.[28]

Despite the divisions in Irish Zionism, the Jewish community remained active members of the respective organisations. The Jewish Representative Council, founded shortly before the Second World War, acted as a liaison between the community and government. However, the minutes of that body for the war years – an important source – have been lost.

During the post-war years, the Irish government under de Valera responded positively to appeals for support for Jewish

113

relief. Although his government had pursued a very illiberal policy towards Jewish refugees during the war, de Valera actively sought to reverse that line in 1945. In 1946, he provided for the sending of kosher meat to Europe. This involved providing work permits for a number of Jewish butchers to travel from the Continent to conduct the slaughter of the animals. All the correct procedures were adhered to in the abattoirs. The meat was tinned and sent abroad for relief purposes.

IRELAND AND THE RECOGNITION OF ISRAEL

Ireland was denied access to the United Nations in the immediate post-war period, and so the Dublin government was very much a spectator as events in Palestine unfolded between 1945 and 1948. In 1945 the British government refused to allow the emigration to Palestine of thousands of Jews who had survived the Holocaust. A report by the UN Special Committee on Palestine, dated 31 August 1947, was adopted as General Assembly Resolution 181(II) on 29 November 1947. It proposed the partitioning of Palestine into Jewish and Arab states, with Jerusalem and the holy places under the direct supervision of the UN. Article 81 of the UN Charter was to be used as the basis for such an international agreement. It was further recommended that Jerusalem – a holy city for three faiths – should be a *corpus separatum* to include the existing municipality of Jerusalem plus a specified surrounding district.[29] The map of the city was drawn to include many outlying areas.

As the interested parties were unable to find a negotiated solution, the armed conflict in the region intensified in 1947 and 1948. Jewish volunteers found their way to Palestine to fight for the cause of an independent state. A number of Irish Jews (the exact number remains to be determined by further research) went to Palestine in those years to participate in the fight to defeat the British forces deployed there under mandate. On the eve of the expiry of the mandate, the state of Israel was proclaimed on 14 May 1948, and a provisional government was established. It fell to David Ben-Gurion to make that proclamation. An Arab–Israeli war followed, and lasted until the beginning of 1949. On 11 May 1949 Israel was admitted to the United Nations. An armistice was signed between Israel and the Arab countries in the summer of 1949. Jerusalem was proclaimed the capital of Israel in 1950; that remains a matter of international dispute.[30] Irish Jews, together with other Jewish communities around the world, received the news of the declaration of a state of Israel with great enthusiasm.

It fell to the inter-party government to handle Irish–Israeli relations in the first two years of the existence of the new state. The minister for external affairs, Seán MacBride, was a member of Clann na Poblachta. That party had been set up in the post-war period to challenge Fianna Fáil and provide the electorate with a 'republican' alternative. A barrister who specialised in the defence of 'republicans', and a former chief of staff of the IRA, MacBride had no previous ministerial or parliamentary experience when he took office in early 1948. Apart from speaking French, his awareness of matters foreign and his understanding of the complexities of international politics remained an unknown quantity. His relative inexperience showed in the indecisive manner in which he handled the question of Irish recognition of the state of Israel. MacBride's temporising must be examined in the light of two factors – Irish partition and, more significantly, Irish popular sensitivities, specifically the concerns of the Catholic hierarchy over international control of Jerusalem and the holy places. The former issue, partition, ought to have been a major factor in contemporary Irish deliberations about the partitioning of Palestine. That was not the case; the issue of control of the holy places took precedence over all other considerations. The Irish government sought to remain close to the position of the Holy See on this matter, and monitored all policy developments in that light. That position was sustained until the late 1950s. Support among Irish Jews for the recognition of the state of Israel remained constant from 1948, but their voice was not powerful enough to change Irish policy.

Many of the major international powers, including the US and the Soviet Union, were quick to recognise the state of Israel. Britain, burdened by a painful recent history of involvement in the region, granted *de facto* recognition on 29 January 1949 and *de jure* recognition on 27 April 1950. Dublin swiftly followed London's lead in the matter of *de facto* recognition, but not that of *de jure* recognition. MacBride sent a telegram on 15 February 1949 to the Israeli minister for foreign affairs, Mose Shertok, giving *de facto* recognition to the state of Israel. A reply was received the following day acknowledging the decision, and conveying the deep appreciation of the Israeli government and the hope for the early establishment of formal relations between the two countries.[31] That hope was to go unfulfilled for many years. *De jure* recognition – much to the disappointment of Irish Jews – did not come until 1963, and the formal exchange of diplomatic relations did not come until 1974. The story of that procrastination was bound up for nearly a decade with Irish government sensitivities over control of the holy places.

ARCHBISHOP McQUAID, IRISH JEWS
AND THE HOLY PLACES

As with anxieties in Dublin over the bombing of Rome during the war years, there were grave concerns in Ireland about damage to the holy places in 1948. There was also a continuous if not growing risk of greater damage to the holy places in a region where protracted peace was unlikely to be established for some time. Irish Catholic concern about the holy places was expressed in its most extreme form in the pages of *Fiat*, a publication issued by Maria Duce. Founded in 1945 by a number of lay Catholics, it had Fr Denis Fahey as its father figure and chief ideologue. A member of the Holy Ghost order, he published widely in the 1930s and 1940s on topics relating to the international power of Freemasons, and the financial and political power of Jews. The subject of Jerusalem and the holy places surfaced frequently in a most strident fashion in the columns of *Fiat*.[32] Maria Duce may have been behind a campaign to get different county councils to submit to government an identical resolution on putting the holy places under international control. During the summer of 1949 the Department of the Taoiseach received resolutions passed by county councils in Limerick, Clare and other counties.[33] The activities of Maria Duce came to the attention of the World Jewish Congress, which appealed on 14 February 1950 to the Jewish Representative Council in Dublin to try to check its influence.[34] The behaviour of Maria Duce was well known to Jewish leaders in Dublin. So strident were its activities to become in the early 1950s – actions that included placing pickets on a theatre in Dublin where Danny Kaye was performing – that the archbishop of Dublin, John Charles McQuaid, used his power to curb its growth. Maria Duce tended to lose momentum from the mid-1950s onwards.

117

Archbishop McQuaid enjoyed ease of access to Irish government departments. He appears to have had a very good informal relationship with the minister for external affairs, Seán MacBride. Irish–Israeli policy and the question of the future of the holy places was an unresolved issue on the desk of the minister at that time. It was also an issue of growing importance in domestic Irish politics. There was evidence that Irish public opinion was becoming agitated about the safety of the holy places. The newly arrived chief rabbi of Ireland, Immanuel Jakobovits, was disturbed by what he found. Because of what the chief rabbi described as 'some mild anti-Jewish demonstrations sparked off by the world-wide agitation on the holy places', he sought a meeting with the archbishop in May 1949. He went to see McQuaid 'in an effort to prevent any serious outbreaks' of hostility towards Irish Jews in Dublin or in other parts of the country. He was accompanied by the chairman of the Jewish Representative Council, Edwin Solomons. Jakobovits explained in his memoirs that he had gone to 'reassure him [the archbishop] of the protection of Catholic rights and property in Israel and to request his assistance in preserving the happy relations between Jews and Catholics in Ireland'.[35]

On 26 May McQuaid wrote a letter to Jakobovits outlining the content of the exchanges. The text of this letter, albeit in draft form, with the archbishop's own handwritten changes, is on file in the records of the Department of External Affairs.[36] McQuaid spoke of the 'sentiment of apprehension among our people', to which he had drawn attention during the meeting:

[It] still persists, and, in my belief, is about to develop. That sentiment, as Mr Solomons – because of his having lived all his life in Dublin – at once appreciated, is very deep and is more widespread than I had first calculated. The apprehension of our people, which is shared by Catholics all over the world, concerns the international status of Jerusalem, the immunity of the Holy Places, not merely of Jerusalem but of Palestine, the rights which, throughout many centuries we have acquired in respect of the holy places, and the opportunity of peaceful access to all the holy places.[37]

McQuaid felt that if the chief rabbi could secure – as he had ventured to suggest – any adequate, firm and authentic guarantees concerning those matters from the Israeli government, this 'would avail much to allay our fears'. The archbishop did not feel that a declaration from the Israeli legation in London could have the same effect as a statement from the seat of the central government. An official declaration from the Israeli government would 'receive wide publicity in Ireland, but, what is equally important, will be carefully noted wherever Irishmen are found, that is, throughout the universe, and especially, in the United States of America'.[38] The archbishop continued:

Such a declaration would greatly assist, too, in preventing unfortunate repercussions, such as you stated you fear may arise in Dublin.

During the war, it was happily possible for me, with the very alert sagacity of Mr Edwin Solomons, to help to forestall incidents which could have provoked retaliation or roused unjust antipathy.

It would indeed be a grievious [sic] *pity, if after having safely traversed a period of world-wide and unexampled crisis, innocent*

> *people of your community should now suffer hurt, by reason of the*
> *attitude and actions of irreligious members of Israeli people, whose*
> *merely political or commercial aims would never be countenanced*
> *by the peaceful members of your community in Dublin.*[39]

McQuaid regarded it as of cardinal importance that Israel should not be seen to be speaking with two voices: on the one hand, giving guarantees in respect of the holy places, and on the other, being 'the voice of a group which seems to have regard only to the seizure and control, for its own ends, of the territory that is for us the Holy Land'.[40] In his journal, published in 1967, Jakobovits quoted the section in italics above and commented:

> In other words, Irish Jews were warned that they would be treated as hostages, be subjected to 'unfortunate repercussions' and would 'suffer hurt' if Catholics were not satisfied with the protection of their interests in Israel. This represents an unprecedented situation in our history. Here is a Jewish community being held accountable and threatened with reprisals for the actions of an independent country, thousands of miles away, for whose policies this community is not responsible and in whose affairs it has no say.[41]

That may have reflected the chief rabbi's immediate reaction to the letter. There is evidence that he wished to go public with the issue; but he was persuaded from doing so by wiser and more prudent counsel in the Jewish Representative Council, whose chairman, Edwin Solomons, had wide experience in the handling of Jewish–Catholic relations.

The sequel to the meeting – details of which may be found

in the archbishop's personal papers – is of interest. Following the meeting, Edwin Solomons intervened with the chief rabbi, expressing his concerns in a letter to McQuaid dated 25 May about the attitude of the Israeli government in reference to the holy places. There had been reports in the national press about a meeting in Galway, where it was held that the Israeli government was not giving freedom of religion, particularly to Catholics. 'As you know, I have many Catholic friends and they were definitely disturbed about these reports', he wrote, adding:

> If these statements are correct it would lead to most serious repercussions in every country, including Ireland. I feel so strongly about the whole matter that some statement should be made without delay; if necessary, someone – you, if it is possible – should go to London. Regarding the appointment of a representative here, the person so appointed must be 'persona grata' to the Irish government and the Catholic Church. It must not be forgotten, about 93% of the population are Catholics.[42]

McQuaid replied on 26 May:

> I am grateful for your note, in which you so kindly let me know your further intervention with the chief rabbi concerning the holy places.
>
> I wish to thank you particularly for your immediate and sympathetic understanding of the whole position. That understanding was very evident on Monday at our meeting.
>
> The chief rabbi is anxious to help to avoid trouble but, if I may say it, he is very young and, as a new appointment in our

country, scarcely appreciates the force of the sentiment that is developing. For instance, you could never have countenanced the publication of his proposed letter. He was a shrewd editor who just said nothing.

I have written to the chief rabbi and, as it is he who should reveal my letter, I would be glad if you would kindly ask him to let you see it. I have but set down my remarks on Monday. Only this may I add: that the feeling of apprehension is not being allayed; on the contrary, it is likely to develop.

You know that I will do all in my power to see to it that the repercussions be not unjust towards your community. It would be a grievous wrong, if the actions of a group of irreligious Israeli people, with mere political and commercial aims to pursue, should cause hurt to innocent people in Dublin, who would never countenance their methods. [43]

Solomons replied to McQuaid three days later:

I am grateful for your friendly, kindly and helpful letter – definite steps are being taken to make what I regard as the most important point, viz. to have a very clear announcement regarding the holy places – Lord Samuel, a distant cousin of mine, gave a broadcast on Friday night – *Palestine Today* – in which he definitely stated that there would be no change regarding free access to the holy places. He has just returned from Palestine. I am writing asking for a copy of the broadcast. I don't know whether he will send same. I will tell him the anxiety we feel here and hope his broadcast is the view of the Israeli government. I saw your letter addressed to the chief rabbi today – I have the impression the chief rabbi realises the urgency of the matter, and will do his utmost. I understand the outlook of my fellow countrymen on this important issue and other matters. It may interest you to know my grandfather, Elias Solomons, came to Dublin from London in 1824. You may rest assured: when I have anything to report, you will have same without delay.[44]

Jakobovits wrote to McQuaid on 31 May:

Whilst the Irish Jewish Community has no means to influence the policy of the state of Israel and cannot, therefore, assume any responsibility for that policy, we shall – as the community which appreciates, and sympathises with, Catholic sentiments probably more than any other – use our best endeavours to elicit from the central government at Tel Aviv a reiteration of its policy for widespread publication – which, I am very glad, you assure me such an official declaration would receive in Ireland – and thus to assist in your efforts at solving the present issue. May I also express my profound gratitude for your generous assurance that the Jewish citizens here can continue to count upon the gracious goodwill of your distinguished self.[45]

McQuaid sent the secretary of the Department of External Affairs, Frederick Boland, a copy of his correspondence with the chief rabbi. The latter replied on 3 June: 'I heard, purely by accident, that the chief rabbi put the letter before his council, and that the question dealt with in it is now receiving the solemn and anxious consideration of the leaders of Dublin's Jewry.' Boland asked whether or not he should send a copy of the letter to Joseph Walshe, who was by this time Irish ambassador to the Holy See.[46] It is not clear whether

that was done or not. But it is likely, at the very least, that Walshe
was made aware in broad outline of the details of the controversy.
On 4 June the archbishop wrote to the chief rabbi acknowledging receipt of a statement made by the Israeli representative to
the United Nations: 'Further, I thank you for your efforts to elicit
from the Tel-Aviv government a statement concerning the due
guarantees of protection for the holy places.' This sequence of letters concluded on 12 June when Edwin Solomons sent McQuaid
a report on the holy places by his kinsman, Lord Samuel. But the
archbishop *did* write on 13 June to Monsignor Gino Paro at the
papal nunciature. He explained that on the day he had received a
letter from Paro, he had discussed the issue of the holy places with
the lord mayor of Dublin and with the minister for finance, Patrick
McGilligan, who had served in the 1920s as minister for external affairs. He had also had a meeting with a Professor O'Brien,
described as a goodwill ambassador from New York.

The professor was of the view that mass demonstration of
Catholics on the issue of the holy places would not be effective in
the US, but did think that Cardinal Spellman 'could affect much
in private with Mr Truman'. The archbishop wrote: 'I fear I cannot
agree with the former point: every manifestation makes for some
good, where Jews are concerned.' McQuaid told Paro that he
would raise the matter with the government, and added: 'I cannot
see *de jure* recognition being accorded to Israel, without definite
guarantees being given concerning the holy places. In this context,
I am constantly in touch with the government.'[47] McQuaid then
went on to relate his exchanges with the chief rabbi:

> It is interesting to record an interview sought by the chief rabbi
> and the lay head of the Jewish community, Mr Solomons. The

latter is a very honourable man, having for acquaintances and friends all his life Dublin Catholics. The chief rabbi is very young.

The chief rabbi was greatly worried by a *Fides* statement on Zionism, and saw the repercussion when the Mansion House was picketed during a Jewish celebration for the foundation of Israel. He had prepared an answer for the *Irish Press*, which the *Press* would not fortunately publish. I advised him to refrain from any such replies and Mr Solomons completely agreed.

During the interview, I made very clear the intense feeling of our people in regard to the holy places and warned the chief rabbi that, if trouble started in Dublin, it would be hard to curtail it. I urged that he use his good offices with the [Israeli] government to give adequate and clear guarantees. He agreed to do what he could to secure guarantees.

The enclosed letter represents my statement to the chief rabbi on the interview we had. The enclosed answer of the chief rabbi is, to a certain extent, satisfactory. The documents which he enclosed are of little value, in my opinion, because they are concerned chiefly with proving the aggression of the Arabs. What is much more valuable is the enclosed copy of a letter sent me by Mr Solomons, with an excerpt from a letter written by his kinsman, Lord Samuel. This much would seem to have been gained: the Jews are realising that a worldwide feeling concerning the holy places is being manifested. And to quote the chief rabbi, when I urged importance of world opinion: 'We Jews,' he declared, 'to put the matter on its lowest basis, have too many hostages in the Christian countries to wish to have trouble in the holy places.' In speaking thus, he put his finger on that which most worries a Jew: the fear of reprisals.[48]

McQuaid repeated at the end of his letter to Paro that he had kept the Irish government informed of these interviews in view of the interest that the government was taking in the holy places.[49]

On 13 July 1949 Seán MacBride outlined in Dáil Éireann Irish policy on Israel and the holy places. He made a special appeal to the government of Israel on the placing of the holy places under an international regime. He felt such an act of generosity would do more than anything else to bridge the gulf between Christian and Jew. That gulf had been responsible down the ages for so much hatred and suffering, and people in Ireland could justly claim to have been more successful in closing the gulf than in most other Christian countries:

> We know how cruelly and unjustly the Jewish people have suffered from intolerance and persecution throughout the centuries. I, personally, am glad that the pages of our history have never been stained with anything of the kind. On the contrary, I think we can claim that our common suffering from persecution and certain similarities in the history of the two races create a special bond of sympathy and understanding between the Irish and Jewish peoples.[50]

The leadership of the Jewish community in Ireland continued to be anxious to help find a way forward on the issue of the holy places. MacBride wrote to Joseph Walshe in Rome on 22 August, and told him that he had been approached by 'a number of prominent Jewish people here who are anxious to know if they could assist in any way'. He had also recently been approached with a view to granting *de jure* recognition to Israel.[51] The issue of *de jure* recognition, as has been mentioned, was not to be resolved until the 1960s. In the interim, the Irish government faced a range of problems arising out of its *de facto* relationship with Israel.

The death of the president of Israel, Chaim Weizmann, on 9 November 1952 presented an unnecessary protocol problem for the Irish government. An External Affairs memorandum noted that on 11 November the minister, Frank Aiken, had addressed a message to his Israeli counterpart conveying sympathy with him, his colleagues and the relatives of Dr Weizmann on the death of their 'great leader and statesman'. The memorandum emphasised that the message had deliberately used the phrase 'your colleagues' instead of 'the government of Israel'. Neither did the statement refer to Weizmann as 'president of Israel' but only as 'great leader and statesman'. The writer raised the question as to whether there should be official representation at a service in the Adelaide Road synagogue in Dublin on 16 November. The protocol was that on such an occasion the president, the government or the minister for external affairs – or all three – could be represented.[52] Iveagh House had advised against the president attending the service: 'It would not seem desirable that the president, who, when he sends a message of sympathy on the occasion of the death of the head of state or other distinguished person, usually conveys not alone his own sympathy but also the sympathy of the people of Ireland, should be represented at this service'.[53] But on the general question of representation, the advice was not so clear-cut:

We have in this country a Jewish community, all or nearly all of whom are Irish citizens and whose relations with their

127

fellow citizens are extremely harmonious. Moreover, a member of the Jewish community, Deputy Briscoe, is a member of Dáil Éireann. Though the Jewish community are nearly all Irish citizens, they, no doubt, feel sympathetically disposed towards the state of Israel and its government, and all of them almost certainly regard the late Dr Weizmann as President of that state and an outstanding leader of the Jewish people everywhere in the world. Doubtless, they would not be displeased if there was some official representation at the Service.[54]

But there was an alternative view: 'We must not overlook the possibility that any official representation at the Service might be unfavourably viewed by a not inconsiderable body of opinion in this country. Indeed, such representation might be liable to be misconstrued and imply a degree of recognition of the state of Israel which we do not accord.'[55]

There was also a query about whether flags would be flown at half-mast on the day of the funeral. 'The question does not now arise since funeral is over', minuted another official. The memorandum also carried a minute dated 11 November 1952: 'Minister will be represented by Deputy Briscoe.'[56] This pedantic approach merely illustrated the silliness of the Irish position of refusing to grant *de jure* recognition to the state of Israel.

THE ROAD TO RECOGNITION

Ireland was admitted to the United Nations in 1956 and took up its position in the General Assembly. The Irish delegation was seated beside that of Israel. However, Irish policy on the recognition of Israel remained something of a backwater in the post-Suez period.

Noël Browne raised the question of establishing diplomatic

World War Two refugees at Rockgrove Camp, Little Island, Co. Cork (01/10/1949). Picture courtesy of *The Irish Examiner*.

L. GOLDBERG,

Offices : 10, Warren's Place, CORK.

Stores : 25, Cattle Market Avenue Shandon St.
and 3, French's Quay,

𝔚𝔥𝔬𝔩𝔢𝔰𝔞𝔩𝔢 𝔞𝔫𝔡 𝔐𝔢𝔱𝔞𝔩 𝔐𝔢𝔯𝔠𝔥𝔞𝔫𝔱.

CURRENT PRICE LIST.

Iron—Mixed

Copper ,,

Brass ,,

Lead ,,

Zinc ,,

Pewter ,,

Woollen Rags

Mixed Rags

Tailors' Clippings

Feathers

Horse Hair

Cow Hair

Curled Hair

N.B.—All Goods to be delivered Free.   Cash by return.

Stationary from Gerald Goldberg's father's store.
Courtesy of the Goldberg Collection, UCC Library Archives Service.

Goldberg with Sheila
through the years.
*Courtesy of the Goldberg
Collection, UCC Library
Archives Service.*

A family group portrait in 'Ben-Truda', the Goldberg home in Cork.
Courtesy of the Goldberg Collection, UCC Library Archives Service.

London, 1949.
Courtesy of the Goldberg Collection, UCC Library Archives Service.

Honorary conferring (UCC 1993).
Courtesy of the Goldberg Collection, UCC Library Archives Service.

Cork Corporation Election
JUNE 18th, 1974

SOUTH EAST WARD

Vote No 1

ALDERMAN

GERALD Y. GOLDBERG
(Non-party)

Printed for the candidate by Hickey & Byrne, Cork

Canvassing leaflet for Corporation election.
Courtesy of the Goldberg Collection, UCC Library Archives Service.

Lord Mayor with An Taoiseach
Captain C. I. Garvey, Chief Officer and Second Officer T. O'Leary
at Centenary Celebration of Fire Brigade.

(Cork Examiner)

Goldberg with then Taoiseach, Jack Lynch.
Courtesy of the Goldberg Collection, UCC Library Archives Service.

Gerald Goldberg.
Courtesy of the Goldberg Collection, UCC Library Archives Service.

Welcoming the Hopiar National Cossack Ensemble from the USSR
for the Cork International Choral Festival. Photo by Richard Mills.
Courtesy of the Goldberg Collection, UCC Library Archives Service.

Goldberg as Lord Mayor. Photo by Tom Matthew Photography.
Courtesy of the Goldberg Collection, UCC Library Archives Service.

Opening of the Trinity Footbridge by Goldberg. This bridge
was renamed by local wags as 'the Passover'. Picture courtesy of
The Irish Examiner'

Dr Aloys Fleischman receiving the Freedom of Cork City from Lord Mayor Gerald Goldberg. Picture courtesy of *The Irish Examiner*.

The hearse bearing the remains of the late Gerald Goldberg, pausing outside the Jewish synagogue on the South Terrace during his funeral (09/02/2004). Picture courtesy of *The Irish Examiner*.

relations with Israel in Dáil Éireann in late 1958. Con Cremin, now secretary of the Department of External Affairs, commented on the deputy's question. He recalled the remark made by Joseph Walshe that the attitude of Pope Pius XII was not entirely shared by other senior Curia officials. 'There may thus be some change in Vatican thinking on the subject', he wrote. On the other hand, Tardini – who had expressed a hard-line position in 1955 to Cremin – had since become secretary of state, 'and such greater influence as this position gives him is hardly calculated to render the Vatican position less rigid'. Cremin did not recommend changing Irish policy towards Israel, and gave Aiken the following argument in favour of retaining existing Irish policy: 'I think that such a step [establishing diplomatic relations] in respect of Israel at the present moment might lead to wrong interpretations on the part of the Arab States and might thus compromise whatever beneficial action we may be able to take in the United Nations towards solving the Arab–Israeli problem.'[57] Frank Aiken took Cremin's advice. The minister told the Dáil on 26 November 1958 that, while he appreciated the desirability of developing cultural, trade and other associations with a number of other countries, he did not think that Dublin would be justified at present in undertaking the additional cost involved in establishing further diplomatic missions.[58]

However, the election of Pope John XXIII helped change the policy of the Holy See towards Israel. Con Cremin changed his own position in the early 1960s on the question of the recognition of Israel. Frank Aiken was also persuaded to change Irish policy. On 10 July 1962 Cremin wrote to the ambassador to the Holy See, T.V. Commins. The secretary referred to the disadvantages of not having given *de jure* recognition to a number of states, mentioning Jordan and Israel by name. Cremin told Commins that the minister proposed to approach the government shortly to accord *de jure* recognition to Israel and Jordan. He was anxious that the Vatican should be made aware of this intention. It was also to be pointed out to the Holy See that it was not Aiken's intention to establish a mission at the present time in either country. The Irish approach was to be made informally.[59]

Commins reported to Dublin on 24 July that he had been assured by a Vatican official that the economic factor involved for the Irish was perfectly understandable and valid, and that Dublin needed to have no fear that Irish action in according *de jure* recognition to Israel would be misinterpreted by the Holy See. Indeed, the Vatican official said, it probably could be argued with some force that the Holy See itself had indirectly given such recognition to Israel by the acceptance of a special ambassador from that country on two occasions – the obsequies of Pope Pius XII and the coronation of his successor, Pope John XXIII – and by the exchange of telegrams between the latter and the president of Israel on the last-mentioned occasion.[60] Neither, he added, would the Holy See have any adverse reaction to the exchange of diplomatic or consular missions if it were so decided. But the Holy See would ask Dublin to ensure that any future diplomatic or consular representative would not reside in Jerusalem or act in any way likely to imply recognition of Jerusalem as the capital of Israel.[61] The anomaly of Ireland's relationship with Israel was at last laid to rest when *de jure* recognition was accorded to that state in 1963.[62]

In December 1974 Ireland and Israel agreed to an exchange of diplomatic representatives. This was to be initially on a non-residential basis. At first, Ireland's representative in Switzerland,

William Warnock, was accredited to Israel. As a matter of conven-
ience, that was changed in 1979 when it was decided to accredit
the Irish ambassador to Greece to Israel. The Irish government
gave approval for the establishment of an Israeli embassy in Dublin
in 1993. Zvi Gabay presented his credentials on 22 July 1995.
Brendan Scannell was appointed as the first resident Irish ambassador to Israel, setting up an Irish embassy in Tel Aviv in 1996.[63]

IRELAND, ISRAEL AND THE SUEZ CRISIS

It is not clear just how many Irish Jews had emigrated to Israel
by the middle of the 1950s. This figure will only be computed
accurately by examining the files in the relevant Israeli government ministries. But the crises in the Middle East in 1956 – Suez
in particular – obliged the Irish government to set in place contingency plans for the evacuation of Irish citizens from Israel.
That was complicated greatly by the fact that the country did
not have any formal representation in Tel Aviv. But the Irish files
reveal a number of very interesting facts about both the Irish in
Israel and the ability of a government to think pragmatically. The
background is as follows. The plight of Irish Jews in Israel was
brought to the attention of the Irish authorities in Dublin by a
letter from J.S. Steinberg, 500 Perdes Hanna, Israel. Writing on 31
March 1956 he addressed his letter to the secretary, Department
of External Affairs:

A chara,
As the political situation in this part of the world grows
more tense, the question of protection of Irish nationals has
arisen. On enquiring at the British Embassy in Tel Aviv, I was
informed that they were not authorised to act on behalf of the

Irish government and that they are accepting registrations of British subjects only. I wonder, therefore, whether it would be possible for some arrangements to be made by which Irish nationals could feel more secure in the event of the situation worsening. I think there are quite a number, especially Irish university graduates, who, while participating in educational and humanitarian work, never forget their loyalty to, and affection for, Ireland.

Mise le meas[64]

Steinberg had already been in contact with the leadership of the Irish Jewish community in Dublin. His initiative, possibly on behalf of other Irish citizens in Israel, had prompted action by the Department of External Affairs. The secretary of the department, Seán Murphy, had phoned the chief rabbi, Immanuel Jakobovits, to get from him the names of Irish Jews living in Israel. Replying on 26 March, Jakobovits told Murphy that he did not have a complete list, nor was he in possession of all addresses. He suggested putting an advertisement in the *Jerusalem Post* requesting Irish citizens to register at a given address. The names supplied by the chief rabbi were as follows:

Mr and Mrs Sol Cantor (and one child)
Mr and Mrs M. Copperman (and two children)
Mr and Mrs H. Finegold
Mr and Mrs J. Jaswon (and one child)
Mr and Mrs N. Jaswon
Mr and Mrs D. Silverstein (and two children)
Mr and Mrs S. Yodaiken (and two children)
Mr and Mrs J.S. Steinberg (and three children)

The chief rabbi felt that the list, though incomplete, included the majority of Irish nationals in Israel. Jakobovits was anxious that arrangements should be made to ensure that, in an emergency, Irish citizens had the same protection and privileges as were enjoyed by other non-Israeli nationals.[65]

According to a later list on departmental files, the names of Irish citizens in Israel were as follows:

Mr H. Orgel, Kiriat Bialik, Haifa

Mr J. Copperman, MA, Pagi, Jerusalem

Mrs Levine (*née* Esther Baker), Rehavia, Jerusalem

Miss Annie Baker, Rehavia, Jerusalem

Mr R.D. Lev, BSc, Bnei Brak

Mr M. Browne, Tel Aviv

Mrs Schwarzman, Talpiot, N. Jerusalem

Dr J. Jaswon, Kfar Hanasi

Mr L. Hyman, MA, 15 Peysner St, Haifa

Mr P. Rifkin, Lavee, near Tiberias

Mr C. Kaye

Dr F.[?] Zuriel (alias Finegold), Tivon

Mr G. Cohen

Rabbi Copperman, 13 Gaza Road, Jerusalem[66]

In a minute to the secretary of the Department of Finance on 7 September 1956, Murphy in External Affairs wrote:

It is not at present possible to give a firm figure for the total number of the persons in these categories [adult Irish citizens in Israel; wives of Irish citizens in Israel; children of Irish citizens in Israel] but such information as the Department has been able to obtain suggests that the figure should not exceed about fifty, comprising about twenty adult males, about fifteen adult females and about fifteen dependent children. The cost of repatriating these persons to Ireland by air, which is the most expensive mode and which might prove necessary, is estimated at approximately 3,400 pounds. The cost of repatriation by land and sea, including a small amount for subsistence, would at the lowest amount to approximately 2,000 pounds.[67]

But that is to jump forward in the process. It would appear that Steinberg acted as a spokesperson in Dublin for the Irish community in Israel. He travelled to Dublin and was interviewed on 12 July 1956 by an official in the Department of External Affairs. His case was very simple: other countries had long before registered their respective nationals and, he assumed, also prepared the necessary travel and transfer arrangements in the event of an emergency. Steinberg stressed that in the event of war, there was no neighbouring country in which Irish citizens in Israel could hope to find refuge. All the surrounding countries, he pointed out, were hostile to Israel. If Irish citizens were obliged to leave Israel, 'they would have to face starting back to Ireland'. He was asked particulars about his own position under Jewish citizenship law:

> He said he was not an Israeli citizen. He was an alien under the law and would have to get a visa for his return to Israel in September. I told him I thought there was some form of easy access to Israeli citizenship made available to returning Jews. Mr Steinberg said there was such a scheme but it had now expired. All returning Jews had to declare themselves as

opting for Israeli citizenship before a certain date; after which, to gain Israeli citizenship, they had to naturalise in the normal fashion and spend a qualifying residence of five years.[68]

Obviously, something had to be done to provide for the contingency of an emergency. But any direct overture to the Israelis would risk the almost certain raising of the question of *de jure* recognition. There was an obvious course of action but it did not recommend itself immediately to the Irish government: Dublin might ask the British government to take care of the interests of Irish citizens in Israel in the event of an emergency. This was discussed at length by the Irish ambassador in London, Frederick Boland, and the secretary of the Department of External Affairs, Seán Murphy. In the end, sensitivities and practical difficulties were overcome.

The Suez crisis concentrated minds in Dublin. On 26 July 1956 Gamal Abdul Nasser announced the nationalisation of the Suez Canal. There was a heightened fear of war in the region. Seán Murphy instructed the London embassy to raise the issue of the protection of Irish citizens in Israel with the relevant British department. An Irish official went to see the assistant under-secretary of the Commonwealth Relations Office, MacLennan, on 21 August 1956. The response was favourable: in principle, the British government was always prepared to take on the protection of Irish citizens whenever Dublin requested it. He saw no reason why there should be any objection in the case of Irish citizens in Israel. MacLennan said he would start the machinery moving immediately. But, in the meantime, his government would require a note formally making the request and indicating the nature and scope of services that might be required.

In order to proceed with arrangements, permission had to be obtained from the minister for finance. Seán Murphy explained in a memorandum dated 7 September 1956 the reason for that course of action. In the light of the international situation, it was proposed that 'subject to the agreement of the Israeli and British authorities, British consular officers in Israel should be authorised to act on behalf of Irish citizens and their dependants there in regard to the provision of consular facilities of an emergency nature, if the necessity arises'. Those facilities were to include the 'transmission to this Department by British Consular officers of requests for passports and passport renewals and endorsements and the subsequent delivery of the passports to applicants; the repatriation of Irish citizens and their dependants from Israel if this proves imperative'.[69] Oral sanction was received from Finance, and the formal written permission was sent to Iveagh House on 26 September. It would appear that the contingency arrangements were put in place.

Happily, it seems no Irish citizen in Israel found it necessary to avail of the contingency arrangements.

MAKING *ALIYA*: A PERSONAL ACCOUNT

David Birkhahn is from Cork. A graduate of UCC, he emigrated to Israel in 1959, where he pursued a distinguished career in dentistry. At my request, he kindly wrote the following account of how he, his brother and his sister made aliya.[70]

The Birkhahns are a third-generation Irish-Jewish family. Solomon Bernard, my grandfather, emigrated from Latvia in 1888 and settled in Cork. His marriage to Rebecca Levin (from Lithuania) was one of the first Jewish weddings in Cork in 1891. While many Jewish immigrants to Ireland in the nineteenth century from the Baltic countries earned their living as pedlars and small-time traders, Solomon Bernard was a herring exporter who operated with his two brothers in Riga and Stockholm.

The family name may have reference to a bird indigenous to the Black Forest in Germany. The name is comprised of two words – '*Birk*', which means 'birch tree' in English, and '*Hahn*', which is the German for 'cock'.

My father's name was Isaac Joseph. He received his licence as a dentist in 1913 having served his apprenticeship in Cork city with Dr George Goldfoot. He started a practice with his brother Ben in the same city. Later, he opened a practice in Bantry and, within a few years, had opened branch practices at Skibbereen, Ballydehob, Schull, Goleen, Castletown, Adrigole and Kenmare. Depending on demand, he attended in those areas once a week, a fortnight or monthly.

I qualified in 1951 at University College, Cork, and went into my father's practice. I made *aliya* in 1959. What follows is my general account of the reasons for Irish emigration to Israel in the 1950s.

While the non-Jewish emigration from Ireland in the 1950s and 1960s was due to the depressed economic situation in the country, a prime factor in Jewish emigration to Israel was the appeal of the Zionist ideology, encouraging resettlement in the historic homeland. The establishment of the state of Israel encouraged large numbers of Jews to emigrate there in the late 1940s and early 1950s. Irish Jews went to Israel in large numbers relative to the size of the local population.

That is not to say, however, that the economic factor was not also a consideration in many cases. There was a dearth of good job opportunities in business and among different professions in Ireland in the 1950s. Moreover, many young Irish Jews wished to live in larger communities of their co-religionists. Israel offered both economic opportunities and the fulfilment of Zionist goals.

The continuing emigration both to Israel and to other countries drained the Irish Jewish communities of leading professional and business people. In the medical profession, approximately twenty physicians and eight dental surgeons settled in Israel in the 1950s and 1960s.

Emigration to Israel was composed mainly of second and third-generation Jews who settled chiefly in the coastal plain from Tel Aviv to Netanya. The professional classes tended to settle in the large cities, while others opted to reside in *kibbutzim* and *moshavim*.

Another generation of emigrants followed the Six Day War in 1967. That event had a profound effect on Jewish communities throughout the world, including Ireland.

Irish Jews who arrived in Israel in the 1950s came to a country where several Irish Jews had already reached positions of prominence in the professions and in public life. Max Nurock was the doyen of Irish Jewry in Israel; he emigrated in the early 1920s. Upon the establishment of the state of Israel in 1948, he joined the Foreign Office and became the Israeli ambassador to Australia.

Bernard Cherrick was vice-president of Hebrew University, and was an influential fundraiser for the university. The late Professor Mervyn 'Muff' Abrahamson was the head of internal medicine at the Rebecca Sieff hospital in Safed. He was also the honorary president of the Israel–Ireland Friendship League.

My brother, Professor Jesmond (Sandy) Birkhahn, was head of anaesthesiology at the Ramban hospital in Haifa for over forty years.

Louis Hyman, born in Dublin in 1912, was a member of the Senate of Trinity College. He settled in Haifa in 1935, and was head of the English department of Hugim secondary school. Hyman's *The Jews of Ireland*, which traced in great detail the immigration of Jews to Ireland from earliest times, immortalised his name and is thus intertwined with the annals of Irish Jewry.

The Herzog family was one of the best known to emigrate to Israel. Chief Rabbi Isaac Herzog was the first chief rabbi of Ireland. In 1936 he received a call to become the first chief rabbi of Palestine.

His two sons, Chaim (Vivian) and Jacob, were notable personalities in Israel. Chaim, who was a lawyer in a prestigious law office, reached the rank of general in the Israeli army, and was also Israel's ambassador to the United Nations; his career was subsequently crowned by his election as president of the state of Israel.

Jacob was appointed to many important government positions: deputy director general of the Foreign Office, director general of the President's Office, and advisor to four prime ministers; as well, he paved the way to the Vatican's recognition of Israel. His debate at McGill University in 1961 with the internationally known historian, Arnold Toynbee, was one of the highlights in a brilliant career that was cut short by his demise in 1972.

All Jewish emigrants from Ireland had influence on other family members. The Coperman family takes pride in the number of emigrants from their family – six. Moshe, an engineer, came on *aliya* in 1950, followed over the years by Rabbi Yehuda, who founded the Jerusalem College for Women; Isaac, a doctor; Gershon and sister Leila. Mrs Sara Coperman also joined her children.

Cork, although it was the home of a small community of about sixty families in the 1950s, boasts of at least two separate (and related) families of six members – the Birkhahns – and four members of the Jackson family. Professor Jesmond (Sandy) Birkhahn and his wife Dorothy emigrated to Israel in 1955; I followed in 1959, and my sister Claire a little later; she was in charge of the Geriatric Division of Public Health in Jerusalem. Our parents, Isaac Joseph and Sophie, emigrated to Israel in 1983.

Additional emigrants included David Jackson, barrister, who emigrated in 1954, followed by his sister Susan, mother Rachel (Ray), and by his brother, Rabbi Edward, who emigrated to Israel upon his retirement as rabbi of Hampstead Garden Suburb Synagogue in London.

The Irish Jewish emigrants have a strong emotional attachment to the country of their birth, and the existence of the Israel–Ireland Friendship League was the outcome of hundreds of Irish Jews settling in Israel. The League was founded in 1969. I was elected founder chairman, and held office until 1998. This organisation holds regular meetings, and seeks to maintain strong intellectual and cultural ties between Ireland and Israel.

Travel Anguish

PAUL DURCAN

A stranger in Belfast,
Alone in the universe,
I am a child astride my mother's shoulder.

In the arrivals hall of David Ben Gurion Airport in Tel Aviv
A little old man in a flaming temper
Is leaping up and down at the hatch of the carousel
Exhorting his baggage to appear.

Despite the solicitous, fraternal warnings of baggage handlers
And of fellow travellers including myself –
(The nerve of me!
I who am always frantic about my baggage!)
The little old man plunges his fingers into the flames –

Into the swaying black drapes of the baggage ovens,
Snatching at bags.

But then when the little old man attempts to climb into the bag-
    gage oven
A youthful rabbi with babe in arms
Who is gazing into the calm, azure eyes of his own smiling wife
Hands over the infant to his wife
And puts his two arms around the little old man, in a loving
    lock.

The baby howls but when the little old man's attaché case
    materialises
And he lifts it up, hugging it, embracing it, feeding it,
The baby smiles and we all stand around and watch
The little old man skip about with his attaché case in his arms.
His newborn babe delivered at last from the flames
In the midst of all these multitudes and signs.

Under the night sky outside the arrivals hall
We are confronted by crowds behind a high wire fence,
Millions of screaming faces in the night clinging to the wire.
I try to turn back but the little old man prods me forward,
Roaring into my ear: 'The important thing is to get out.'

Outside the wire,
On the perimeter of the screaming crowd,
He urinates into the grass,
Patriarchal piss.
He is all overcoat lapels,

Giving his breast to the universe,
Repeating his message to me:
'The important thing is to get out.'

Pointing me in the direction of the Jerusalem bus,
And buttoning up his fly,
He puts his two hands up to his star-shaped lapels,
And twirling his two wrists round his breasts,
Lays his head on his left shoulder, and sideways bows to me.
I take my leave of him, bold for my journey.

A stranger in the Holy Land,
Alone in the universe,
I am a child astride my mother's shoulder.

'Dabru Emet': Its Significance for Jewish–Christian Dialogue[1]

RABBI DAVID ROSEN

In 2000 a Jewish statement on Christians and Christianity entitled 'Dabru Emet' (Speak the Truth) was published, having been endorsed by more than 200 rabbis and scholars from different streams of contemporary Judaism. Almost all signatories were American. (That the statement had been prepared under the auspices of the Baltimore Institute for Christian and Jewish Studies guaranteed its Americanocentricity.) It was advertised in the *New York Times* and *Baltimore Sun*, and was widely seen and acknowledged.

Media coverage is only a partial explanation for the degree of excitement that the statement generated in Christian circles right across the world, and many of us were very much surprised by how strong the positive reaction was. Though I was among those who signed 'Dabru Emet' (one of the few non-Americans), I did not consider the text to be unusually far-reaching. I believed that the Jewish perspectives in the International Council for Christians and Jews (ICCJ) Theology Committee's statement, *Jews and Christians in Search of a Common Religious Basis for Contributing Towards a Better World*,[2] for example, go further than 'Dabru Emet'. However, these comparative institutional sour grapes, or questions as to why other statements are not as well known, are not important. What is significant is the undeniable fact that 'Dabru Emet' was received in public addresses and articles by people of no less stature than Cardinals Kasper and Keeler, the Protestant scholar Walter Bruegemann, and Archbishop George Carey of Canterbury, not only as an historic document, but as ushering in a new era in Christian–Jewish relations.

This response clearly revealed just how profound and unsatisfied the need in Christian circles engaged in and committed to dialogue with the Jewish community was for some public Jewish declaration of reciprocity, in response to the far-reaching theological changes that had taken place over the last forty years in Christian attitudes and teaching regarding Jews and Judaism. This reaction alone was eloquent justification and vindication of 'Dabru Emet'.

That it seemed to satisfy an apparently unmet need would perhaps suggest that suspicions prevailed in Christian circles that the attitudes very much associated with two modern Orthodox American rabbis – Eliezer Berkowitz and J.B. Soloveitchik – and thinkers of the previous generation were still widely held within the Jewish community. (Both rabbis were, relevantly, refugees from Europe.) Berkowitz's position was simple and consistent: the Christian world had done us too much harm for too long – having facilitated if not collaborated with the worst horrors of Jewish experience – to put the past behind us so easily. If Christians wanted authentic Jews to respond positively to their overtures, Christians would have to demonstrate the genuineness of their respect and goodwill towards the Jewish community over a few generations before a positive Jewish response would be possible.

Rabbi Soloveitchik's position was both more sophisticated and less consistent. His argument was that Jews and Christians were 'two faith communities [that are] intrinsically antithetic', and that it was not possible to share insights that are exclusively part of one's subjective spiritual experience. Accordingly, he ruled out any 'theological' dialogue, though he acknowledged that on humanitarian issues such as war and peace, poverty, freedom, morality, civil rights and the threat of secularism, 'communication among the various faith communities is desirable and even essential'. It has been suggested that Soloveitchik was actually trying to give a permissive ruling so that modern Orthodox participation in Jewish–Christian meetings was possible at all! This may have been the case, but Soloveitchik's ruling is now always interpreted restrictively, and not permissively.[3]

Moreover, whatever his motive may have been, Soloveitchik revealed his rationale behind this position. It emerged out of his own profound sense of alienation in the world, a perception that was central to his existential approach to life. He may well have reflected the mind-set of many Orthodox Jews in this regard, though I suspect that paradoxically it would resonate primarily with an orthodoxy that does not call itself 'modern'. He described

the relationship between Jews and Christians as the relationship of 'the few and weak vis-à-vis the many and the strong',
and appealed to friends within the Christian 'community of the
many' to respect 'the right of the community of the few to live,
create and worship in its own way, in freedom and with dignity'.[4]
Soloveitchik thus revealed that his fears were the traditional
Jewish trepidations born out of past bad experience: begin with
theological dialogue and it will soon become polemic or at least
an unconscious vehicle for the strong and many to impose themselves upon, and even undermine, the weak and few!

An effective critique of this position was provided in an article in 1977 by the late Orthodox Jewish scholar, Professor Zvi
Yaron.[5] Yaron questioned the legitimacy of such a perspective
in the contemporary context, especially as Soloveitchik himself acknowledged 'the threat of secularism', which is really the
dominant contemporary ethos in Western society. Today, in the
West particularly, all religions are minorities and are vulnerable
(though that vulnerability and minority status actually has its own
empowerment). Above all, however, Yaron criticised Soloveitchik's
complete omission of any reference at all to the state of Israel,
which indeed is strange given Soloveitchik's unquestionable commitment to it. To be sure, the fulfilment of the Zionist vision
that has placed the Jewish people in a very different position in
our world undermines the very basis of Soloveitchik's perspective.
Yaron effectively criticised Soloveitchik's theological exclusivity,
through exposing the contemporary inappropriateness of the ter-
minology and categories that Soloveitchik used to promote his
thesis.

However, the position may also be criticised for its ontological
self-contradiction. As the prophet Malachi points out (chapter

3, verse 16), even when people of faith just talk to each other, it is of theological consequence. It is artificial and simply incorrect to suggest that in addressing issues of humanitarian concern, we are not concerning ourselves with 'doctrinal, dogmatic or ritual aspects of our faith'. If we do not oppose entirely the deepening of positive Jewish–Christian relations, but on the contrary wish to encourage these, then inevitably we are in the business of exchanging and sharing theological insights and affirmations even in the midst of addressing common humanitarian concerns, and we would do well to approach these seriously rather than play games pretending to be 'outside', as it were, when we are already engaged in dialogue. 'Dabru Emet' certainly demonstrated the unequivocal repudiation of such negative attitudes towards Jewish–Christian dialogue by the widest cross-section of Jewish religious and academic leadership. As obvious as this was to those of us in the Jewish community engaged in this field, evidently it had not been so to very many of our Christian collaborators, and as I have said, that in itself gave the statement great value.

The Christian excitement related firstly to the fact that this public Jewish statement recognised Christians and Christianity today as not being the same as they were in the past; that Christianity today is not only no longer principally a threat to Judaism, but is in fact substantially an ally. It also related to the fact that the statement recognised a Jewish interest not only in a social and moral relationship with Christianity, but also in a relationship of theological understanding between the two. In effect, 'Dabru Emet' represents a Jewish willingness not to forget, but to put behind us the unique, tragic past that bedevilled the Jewish–Christian relationship, and to look forward to a unique, fraternal, theological interaction in the future. Indeed, the statement was criticised in certain Jewish quarters precisely on both these grounds.

There are those who, while they do not share Berkowitz's rejectionism, do believe that the declaration lets Christianity off the hook too easily, too early. These reservations focus on the passage in 'Dabru Emet' that rejects the idea of laying the blame for past Christian anti-Semitism and anti-Judaism at the door of contemporary Christians (an ironic reversal of Christian charges against Jews!), and declares that 'Nazism was not a Christian phenomenon', even if it succeeded to the extent it did as a result of Christian anti-Semitic attitudes. The passage goes on to declare that 'if the Nazi extermination of the Jews had been more successful, it would have turned its murderous rage more directly to Christians.' (As early as 1941, the renowned American Jewish writer, Maurice Samuel, argued in his book, *The Great Hatred*, that Nazi venom towards the Jews was in effect an expression of its hostility towards the essence of Christianity itself.[6]) One may dispute this theory, but I do not believe, however, that a fair-minded person could dispute the central thesis that Nazism was not a Christian phenomenon in and of itself. Of course, if this had been a Christian statement, then we would have expected some extensive soul-searching and greater acknowledgement of the sin of Christian anti-Semitism. But 'Dabru Emet' is a Jewish statement and is explicitly directed at Jews. The Jewish community does not need persuading as to the case of Christian historic guilt and responsibility for anti-Semitism. As a modern Jewish leader in dialogue with Christianity has put it, the Jewish community often tends to indulge in a 'triumphalism of pain'.[7] Inevitably, one must then conclude that the Jewish criticism of this clause is motivated by what I describe above as an unwillingness to let contemporary

Christians off the historical hook. I would consider this a perhaps legitimate Jewish 'hang-up' – after all, anti-Semitism is still very much a reality – as it allows subjective historical experience or pain to be the moral criterion and arbiter, rather than individual responsibility. (Of course, the motive could be far worse, namely a desire to nurture in order to manipulate Christian guilt!)

The other main Jewish criticism of 'Dabru Emet' has focused on the theological affirmation of Christianity, especially the phrase 'Jews and Christians worship the same God'. We might at the outset point out that Judaism – or certainly the Hebrew Bible – does not engage in theological speculation; does not contain a catechism; nor does it even make doctrine a determinant factor in worship. Indeed, to serve or worship God is defined precisely as 'walking in His ways', 'observing His commandments'. In other words, the basic criterion for determining whether we worship God or not is our religio-ethical conduct. Moreover, the unique Divine self-designation in the book of Exodus ('I am that which I am', or, more literally, 'I shall be that which I shall be') has been understood precisely to mean that no two people have the same conception of the Divine. Indeed, even within any one tradition and denomination, one will find very differing perceptions of the Deity. Sometimes, there are serious divergences, if not conflicts, over such understandings. Rabbi Shlomo MinHahar of Provence, for example, considered certain of the theological principles of Maimonides to be heretical.[8] But neither intended that the other did not worship the same God. Similarly, within my own contemporary Jewish orthodoxy, there are colleagues of mine who maintain theological conceptions that I find unacceptable, but I do not think that they are worshipping another Deity! Certainly, our faiths have defined limits to pluralism and

theological diversity, but it is actually not at all necessarily contradictory to affirm that someone worships the same God and at
the same time contend that the other's perception of the Deity is
problematic and/or flawed.

Moreover, those who have criticised this phrase in 'Dabru
Emet' appear to have ignored the dominant view of 'chachmei
Ashkenaz' (the medieval rabbinic sages in Christian lands),
that even though Christian faith affirmations compromise pure
monotheism, this does not prevent them from coexisting with
Judaism's truth affirmations: these ideas do not make Christianity
idolatrous. Moreover, some of the most pre-eminent rabbis of
their times – such as Menachem HaMeiri, Moses Rivkes, Jacob
Emden, Elijah Benamozegh and Israel Lifschitz – viewed
Christianity not only as ethical monotheism but attested to the
religio-ethical redemptive role of Christianity in human society,
often in language and ideas far more bold than in 'Dabru Emet'.
Indeed, in stating that Christianity has brought 'hundreds of millions of people … into relationship with the God of Israel', and
has led them to 'accept the moral principles of Torah', 'Dabru
Emet' simply echoes statements within the writings of the afore-
mentioned rabbinic authorities and many others over the course
of the last millennium.

Perhaps the most far-reaching call of 'Dabru Emet' is for Jews
'to respect Christians' faithfulness to their revelation' (which, inci-
dentally, is an almost verbatim quote of Martin Buber's words in
his article, 'The two foci of the Jewish soul', published in 1948).
This expression of theological respect and its dialogic implications would seem to highlight a principal source of Christian
excitement over 'Dabru Emet'. In effect, the excitement reflects
a perceived development of a Jewish theology of Christianity. In

this regard, it might be more correct to describe 'Dabru Emet' less as the substance and more as a sign.

As indicated, a positive theological understanding of Christianity is not a new thing. It was arguably Emden who was the most influential of rabbinic authorities in this regard. In addition to acknowledging Jesus' commitment to Torah and his mission to strengthen that commitment within the people of Israel, he also expresses appreciation of the fact that through the message of Jesus' ministry, Christianity has brought about the widespread elimination of idolatry.[9] However, Emden goes far further in describing Christianity in the language of the Mishnah in Pirkei Avot as '*knessiah leshem shamayim*', i.e. a gathering for the sake of Heaven. (However, the Hebrew word '*knessiah*' is also used precisely to mean 'church' [building].) Such a body is described by the Mishnah as being of permanent value, sanctifying the Divine name. Emden accordingly portrays Christianity in terms of Divine purpose and value.

Indeed, a serious Jewish theology of Christianity will need to go further than simply respecting 'Christians' faithfulness to their revelation'; it requires an understanding of the significance of that revelation in terms of the Divine plan for humanity. It may be said that in the early twentieth century, Jewish philosophers – most notably Franz Rosenzweig and to a lesser degree Martin Buber – sought to develop this idea further; but it was still on the basis of viewing Christianity as the Divine message to the Gentiles, rather than offering any insight that could be of any value for Judaism. However, the remarkable strides in Jewish–Christian relations over the last four decades have produced a new openness to such. These have included seeing Judaism and Christianity in a mutually complementary role in which the Jewish focus on the communal covenant with God and the Christian focus on the individual relationship with God may serve to balance one another. Others have seen the complementary relationship in that Christians need the Jewish reminder that the Kingdom of Heaven has not yet fully arrived, while Jews need the Christian awareness that in some ways that Kingdom has already rooted itself in the here and now. Another view of mutual complementarity portrays Judaism as a constant admonition to Christianity regarding the dangers of triumphalism, while Christianity's universalistic character may serve an essential role for Judaism in warning against degeneration into insular isolationism. Opposed to the underlying assumptions of the latter is the contention that it is actually Christianity's universalism that jars with a culturally pluralistic reality in the modern world. The communal autonomy that Judaism affirms may serve more appropriately as a model for a multicultural society, while Christianity may provide a better response for individual alienation in the modern world.

In addition, Jewish as well as Christian theologians have written about the mutual theological assistance Jews and Christians can provide one another in overcoming the burdens of history. It has also been pointed out that Jewish–Christian reconciliation itself has impacted on society well beyond the bilateral dialogue. Accordingly, it serves both as a universal paradigm of reconciliation and should serve as an inspiration for Jews and Christians for dialogue, especially with Islam and even beyond in the multi-faith encounter.

Indeed, as mentioned earlier, even the widespread acceptance that our shared ethical values and moral responsibilities demand our cooperation and collaboration – today more than ever before as we face the challenges provided by the dominant secular culture in which all religions are minorities – has theological implications for our relationship. Pope John Paul II[10] expressed this beautifully when he observed that 'Jews and Christians are called (as the Children of Abraham) to be a blessing for humankind. In order to be so, we must first be a blessing to one another.' What then are the theological implications of such mutual blessing?

All these ideas reflect the real theological challenge that we who labour in love in this vineyard of Jewish–Christian relations are called to address with increasing candour and depth. How may we understand not only each other's integrity as each defines one's self, but furthermore understand each other's role accordingly in the Divine plan for humanity and understand our relationship in these terms? What is God saying to us in this regard, and how may we benefit from one another – indeed, becoming a blessing to one another in the deepest sense possible?

Perhaps then, the excitement with which 'Dabru Emet' was received reflected the fact that there is now a genuine search for answers to these questions within both communities.

From *Shoa* to *Shalom*: The Case for Abolishing War in the Twenty-first Century

ENDA McDONAGH

THE SETTING

In his exhibition in Galway, in August 2003, the Irish sculptor, John Behan, exhibited an elegant bronze of one of his favourite and most attractive subjects – birds – entitled *Doves on Fence*. How far the irony is intentional only he can explain. For people increasingly opposed to war as a justified moral solution to a political problem – being 'doves' as distinct from 'hawks' – the fence-sitting itself, refusing to engage with the problems that provoke war and with the need to seek alternatives, are no longer morally justified.

This essay by an Irish Catholic theologian in a work honouring an Irish Jewish lawyer, Gerald Goldberg, is also written in painful consciousness of the fence-sitting (at best) of so many Europeans, Catholic and other Christians, during the 1930s and 1940s when Gerald Goldberg's fellow Jews were facing extinction. In that spirit, the title, 'From *Shoa* to *Shalom*', is intended to explore how such catastrophes must not only be avoided (*nie wieder*), but replaced by a version of the great Hebrew vision and promise of *Shalom*, which might be best translated not simply as peace but as 'flourishing together in community', comprising eventually the whole human community.

A further word on the origins of the theme. After some years of gestation, the American theologian, Stanley Hauerwas, of Duke University, Durham, North Carolina, and this author composed an 'Appeal to Theologians and Religious Leaders' to work for the abolition of war and the development of alternatives during the twenty-first century. The appeal was presented at conferences at the University of Notre Dame, Indiana, in September 2002, and at Maynooth in November 2002, and has been published subsequently.[1] This essay is to some extent an expansion of that appeal, with much more attention to traditional arguments for a just war, to the difficulties that any alternative has to face, and to the process and stages by which such an alternative might be introduced.

The controversy over the justification of the 2003 invasion of Iraq, before and after its occurrence, has given a fresh edge to the debate and a new relevance to the project of abolishing war. Similar ideas and movements are beginning to develop around the world among ordinary people, politicians and even military personnel, as well as among the 'usual suspects' of pacifists, radical

Christians, women's groups and other political activists. The Irish Anti-War Movement, which was at the centre of organising the protest against the recent war in Iraq and which published the interesting volume, *Irish Writers Against the War*, also states: 'We want to play our part in building the international movement to stop all wars.' This has been the long-standing ambition of Pax Christi, Ireland, together with its international associates.

On the basis of his criticism of the war in Iraq and his stringent efforts to prevent it, Pope John Paul II would seem to come very close to outlawing all war in the present world context. His phrase in the encyclical, *Centesimus Annus* (1991), 'War never again' – an exact echo of Pope Paul VI's remark at the United Nations in 1967 – suggests that at that level of leadership, the Catholic Church may be committing itself to the abolition of war as a moral instrument in extreme circumstances. For such a stance to be credible, Church leaders, in common with all other promoters of the abolition of war, will have to devote time and resources to the elaboration of alternatives and to the persuasion of its members who are also influential as citizens, politicians and military.

This, however, is not another appeal by a theologian to religious leaders or theologians, whatever their value in the overall project. One significant theologian in the debate, Professor Hans Kung of Tübingen, has argued that there can be no peace between the nations without peace between the religions. In many parts of the world, from Northern Ireland to the Middle East to South-east Asia and beyond, this argument seems to have much validity. The more central concern here is to examine the continuing usefulness and validity of just-war theory and practice in today's globalising world, and the feasibility of providing other solutions to the neuralgic problems of national security and sovereignty, of local conflict and global terrorism.

Writing in an Irish setting in honour of a distinguished Irish citizen, it is impossible to avoid the topic of Irish neutrality. Without engaging with the tangled history of the underlying theory and actual practice of Irish neutrality, it may be that the implications of the abolition project may allow an Irish foreign policy that honours both its traditional stance of neutrality – still cherished, it seems, by very many Irish citizens – and its new commitments to European security and global peace. At least, this is worth considering in face of the emotional and divisive controversy that some unimaginative proposals for dismantling neutrality and some rigid interpretations in retaining it may provoke.

JUST WAR AND ITS LIMITATIONS

The 'just-war theory' is not in its origins Christian. It existed at least in embryonic form and in varying versions among the Hebrew prophets, as well as among the Greek and Stoic philosophers. It was known to Greek, Roman and other political and military leaders prior to its adoption by Christians in the fourth century of the Common Era (CE). There is a certain irony in its adoption, and particularly in its widespread propagation by Christians, given that in their first three centuries they had rejected war and bearing arms as contrary to the teaching and example of their founder, Jesus Christ.

Several summary conclusions may be drawn from the long and controversial development of just-war theory and practice within the (Christian) West over 1,500 years. The arguments about just war became increasingly complicated in face of the increasing complexity of military arms and their modes of delivery, from hatchets and spears to bows and arrows, from guns and cannonry to bombs (conventional, atomic and nuclear), and from foot soldiers to horses and battleships, from motor vehicles to tanks, and from jet fighters and bombers to rocket launchers. Medieval debates about the moral legitimacy of bows and arrows were mirrored in similar debates about the use of gunpowder centuries later, continuing to the latter-day debates about cluster bombs and landmines, atomic, biological and chemical weapons. While the moral hesitations and debates about new weaponry may have had some restraining influence from time to time – as theologians and moralists attempted to refine the traditional *jus in bello* which presumed to impose moral limits on the actual conduct of war – morality and international law usually arrived too late, reflecting, like the infamous generals, the lessons of the last wars rather than examining in detail the new challenges of current or imminent wars.

Allowing for the later arrival of many moral and legal restrictions on the conduct of war, it remains sadly true that few if any historical wars have abided by the already established canons of morality or legality in the conduct of war. The best-case scenario of recent times, the Second World War as undertaken and conducted by the Allied forces against the Nazi and fascist regimes, led, it is frequently asserted, through the carpet bombing of German cities and the atomic bombing of Japanese cities, to clear violation of the respect for non-combatants demanded by one traditional criterion for just conduct in war. It is at least debatable how far claims for precision bombing and the euphemistic invocation of unavoidable collateral damage in recent wars have given much real protection to non-combatants, especially when there have also been hospitals, communication centres, bridges and other civilian installations directly targeted and destroyed. One fairly safe generalisation from the history of wars might be that there never has been a war in which non-combatants have not been extensively killed and wounded. On that criterion alone, wars have proved mainly unjust and perhaps unjustifiable. The qualifiers 'mainly' and 'perhaps' will be considered later in discussing some of the other criteria.

The counterweight to *jus in bello* was and is *jus ad bellum*. For many defenders of just war. this is the primary and, for some, the only significant criterion for a just war. In the fourth and fifth centuries CE, when the Christian theologian-bishops, Ambrose and Augustine, were pioneering the Christian theological justification of war and urging Christians to join the imperial armies, their argument was based on the need to defend neighbours – Roman citizens – against the fearsome incursions of the barbarians who later managed to sack Rome itself. Defence against unjust and deadly aggression was their just cause, and the first criterion advanced in moral argument. In his classic historical-theological analysis of just-war theory over the centuries, Princeton theologian, Paul Ramsey, proposed, with considerable scholarly acuity, that the fourth-century change in Christian theory and practice, and its subsequent development, arose out of the Hebrew and Christian command of love of neighbour, with the consequent entailment to protect her/his life against unjust aggressors. Even in the tumultuous days of the Vietnam War, and of the opposition to it, Ramsey stayed with his love of neighbour and her defence as justifying war. Today's Western rhetoric in support of particular wars is seldom far removed from that sentiment, even if the language is more of defence of freedom than of love of neighbour.

The justice of the cause has been the primary criterion in seeking to justify going to war, but it has been gradually qualified by a number of related criteria. These involve what is nowadays called proportionality between the evil threatened and that which will inevitably ensue in war and, by reasonable prediction, may be expected to follow the war. Too often, war has simply bred more war, and that lesson seems very difficult for political and military leaders to absorb. How far did the Great War and its resolution at Versailles lead to the rise of Nazism and so to the catastrophes of the Second World War and of the Holocaust? The success of that war in ending the Nazi and fascist tyrannies was clearly not of obvious benefit to the Poles, for example, whose invasion by Nazi Germany prompted the Allied declaration of war. It must also be remembered that protection of the Jews faced with genocide played little or no role in the declaration and conduct of the war despite growing awareness of the threat to the Jews through the 1930s and into the war years. All this emphasises the ambiguities of war in its initiation, continuance and conclusion.

Just cause as primary criterion is also restricted by the demand to engage in war only when all other means of averting the existing or threatened evil have been exhausted. This is obviously not an easy judgement to make, as the heated and inconclusive debates about inspections of Iraq's weapons of mass destruction, their threat to their neighbours or to the wider world, and how best to deal with any such threat, made clear in the spring of 2003. In a more dynamic view of 'last resort', commitment to extend alternative means to war now and into the future might at least give further pause to the trigger-happy who are easily seduced by the prospect of 'shock and awe' solutions to long-existent and near-intractable problems. Again, the aftermath of military victory in Iraq suggests alternatives might have been more earnestly and imaginatively sought and the likely consequences more fully thought through before the decision to go to war was finally made.

In this context, the prospect and meaning of success in war enter into the equation. What should count as success in a particular war? Saving a small country like Poland from a tyrannical neighbour? Preserving the people of Vietnam from the horrors of communism? Discovering and destroying Saddam's weapons of mass destruction? Change of regime in Iraq? Liberating the Iraqi people? Promoting peace and democracy in the region? Further victory in the 'war against terrorism'? Securing Western interests, particularly in relation to oil? All of these questions about recent wars do not admit of ready, and certainly not agreed, answers even among Allied states and statesmen. They do, however, serve to underline again the ambiguities of war in its intentions and achievements, and whisper, at least, 'there must be a better way'.

Beneath and beyond the whispering, there is a growing belief and increasing clamour that human beings must find alternatives to war in resolving political conflict and providing for human security. This widespread conviction is no longer satisfied with the niceties of just-war theory and the awfulness of its practice. For many thoughtful people around the world, war is the last of the great social barbarisms, and should follow slavery, torture and other historical barbarisms into moral and legal oblivion. Before that can happen, a great deal of careful social and political analysis as well as innovative and creative social and political change in mind-set, structure and practice will be demanded. No one essay, indeed no one theoretical dissertation, however lengthy, could hope to chart such analysis and change. In these matters, praxis frequently anticipates theory, experimentation settled programmes. All that will take time. The hope must be that the twenty-first century will witness the abolition of war as a moral and lawful instrument of politics, as the nineteenth century witnessed the abolition of slavery as a moral and lawful instrument of economics. The continuing existence of slavery or enslavement in disguised or more limited forms does not give it any legal respectability or protection. One can no longer use as a legal or moral defence the concept of 'just slavery'. No doubt, political recourse to arms in disguised or limited fashion will continue also, but without the protection of international law or traditional morality.

ALTERNATIVES: THEIR FOUNDATIONS, THEIR POSSIBILITIES AND THEIR DIFFICULTIES

In the appeal to theologians and others, the arguments for the abolition of war were primarily religious and, given the theologians involved, mainly Christian. As indicated earlier, this is a different kind of essay. However, any discussion on war and its alternatives has to take account of the formative religious traditions of Judaism and Christianity, particularly in the Western world, home and source of the most destructive weaponry and war the world has known. The God to whom Gideon in the Book of Judges dedicates an altar as to the Lord of Peace (Jud 6:24) is hymned most beautifully in Psalm 84:

I will hear what the Lord God has to say,
a voice that speaks of peace,
peace for his people and his friends
and those who turn to him in their hearts.

Mercy and faithfulness have met;
justice and peace have embraced.
Faithfulness shall spring from the earth
and justice looks down from heaven.

The Lord will make us prosper
and our earth shall yield its fruit.
Justice shall march before him
and peace shall follow his steps.

The close connections revealed here between the ambitions of the Lord for His people and His Creation and the corresponding Divine and human attributes – peace, justice, mercy, loving kindness, faithfulness, prosperity and fruitfulness of the earth – summarise the characteristics of the Messianic age so often announced by the prophets. And the key feature of that age is *Shalom*, the fullness of peace, the state of humanity flourishing together in community. All of this in ambition and actuality is of course still embedded in a sinful and destructive world until the Messiah comes and the Reign or Kingdom of God is finally established.

For Christians, the Messiah has already come in Jesus Christ. The Reign of God is at hand. It has been established in principle for all people, but must be accepted in love and pursued in practice by all justice-seekers and peacemakers who are addressed as disciples by Jesus in his charter for the Reign of God – the Sermon on the Mount – and in other passages and parables. For many Christians over the millennia, Jesus' teaching was enough to outlaw war, while they sought with more or less energy and success to devise alternatives. In the present debate, such Christians need no other authority for their opposition to war, while ironically many followers of the one God/Yahweh/Allah, through adherence to Moses, Jesus and Mahomet in the three Abrahamic faiths, may be the most resistant to the proposal to abolish war.

In the course of the twentieth century, three very religious people led the way in theory and practice in the search for alternatives to violence and war in opposing the oppression of their peoples and providing the freedom so rhetorically in vogue in the West. Beginning with Gandhi in the 1890s in South Africa, and later in India, emerging in mid-century in the US with Martin Luther King, and reaching a climax in the Republic of South Africa in the 1990s with Nelson Mandela, the philosophy and political strategy of non-violent defence of neighbour, and restraint of the armed aggressor and oppressor, opened up new possibilities of achieving justice, freedom and security for all kinds of people.

Gandhi, the most original thinker and actor among these leaders, drew on his own Hindu tradition with its enormous respect for all living creatures, on Jesus' Sermon on the Mount and its teaching of love of enemies, and on the broader moral traditions with their emphasis on truth, justice and freedom. His priority on firmness in the truth (*satyagraha*) as the counter to armed force or violence was put to the test many times by himself and his *satyagrahi* – those who stood firm in the truth and refused to meet violence with violence. '*Emeth*', the Hebrew word for truth and faithfulness in truth – a particular characteristic of Yahweh and his loyal people – has much in common with Gandhi's concept and practice of *satyagraha*. Neither has much in common with the propaganda and spin of warring nations. The old adage retains its validity: the first casualty of war is truth. Gandhi's belief and his partial achievement was that by continuing to expose the truth of violence, oppression and injustice such as that experienced by Indians and Africans at the hands of their white masters, and by enduring the suffering that attempts to expose and uphold that truth would inevitably bring, the masters would be eventually compelled by public disapproval, national and personal shame, if not by conscience, to desist from their violence. In pursuit of his goals, Gandhi realised that his *satyagrahi* needed careful preparation and training if they were to survive the rigours of the campaign and resist the temptation to counter-violence. Beyond that, he was as calculating a strategist in planning his exposure campaigns, protest marches and fasting periods as any military general. The limited but undoubted success his campaigns achieved in the liberation of India revealed the strengths and weaknesses of such a programme in face of deep ethnic and religious divisions, and of the usual practice of empire in exploiting such divisions to retain mastery. Gandhi's insight that a successful programme such as his would lead to mutual emancipation for British master as well as Asian underling was too much for most of his contemporaries, Indian perhaps as well as British. And it exposes another harsh dimension of the war-game, the dehumanising effect it has on the players, from generals in their combat centres to foot soldiers on the ground. The false heroics of war were well known to Gandhi from the horrors of the Great War. His firmness in the truth would expose the falsity of all such glorifying of war, and liberate both sides into possibilities of reciprocal justice and peace.

While Gandhi's vision and practice inspired to good effect such powerful disciples as Martin Luther King and Nelson Mandela and, indeed, John Hume and colleagues in Northern Ireland, it has yet to capture much support in the West among the political classes. Of course, it would not on its own be adequate to the long, slow process of providing alternatives to war around the globe. It could prompt the first essential step, the change in mind-set that is so badly needed among the warrior-political classes that tend by inclination or indifference to dominate discussion of issues such as freedom and security. Interestingly, justice seldom figures in the vocabulary of these people, still captive to the old Roman imperial tag: *si vis pacem, para bellum* – if you desire peace prepare for war. Talk of defending by war the 'Free World' in such a deeply unjust world is as misleading as it is futile. For the coming non-imperial times, for which one hopes, the new tag might read: *si vis pacem, para justitiam* – if you desire peace, prepare for justice. That is the change in mind-set that is immediately required. No peace without justice and, finally, no justice without peace.

Changing mind-sets at leadership and popular level will be slow and painful, and always incomplete. It will be helped by short-term strategies to relieve glaring injustices between developed Western countries and the developing or impoverished countries of Africa, Asia and Latin America. This will involve changes in economic structures and practices that will demand serious commitment to fair trade in ways not yet shown by the economic powers, as well as the political will to impose such fairness if necessary. All the while, international institutions will need to be strengthened in ways that ensure a growing body of just international law and effective means for its enforcement. These recommendations, which could and should be extended by the relevant experts, may appear at best obvious and banal, or at worst naive. What about national security? Humanitarian interventions? Disarmament and the elimination of the arms trade and industry?

And so on. All these must be addressed and acted upon in ways that avoid, prevent or at least reduce in the short term the horror and inhumanity all war involves. Time and patience certainly, no easy and quick fix, but commitment and urgency also for the sake of the next, and the next, and the next ... who may die of war or injustice or both.

In seeking to move on from war and genocide to a just and peaceful human community – from *Shoa* to *Shalom* – mistakes will be made by so-called realists and idealists. It is difficult sometimes to tell the one from the other. Are the so-called hawks of world politics really realists? Do their understandings of the world and their prescriptions for its development and security offer any real hope of success? Are they simply idealists, those who would, mind by mind, structure by structure, practice by practice, day by day, month by month, year by year and decade by decade, seek the promotion of justice, the reduction and eventual elimination of political violence apart from the international police forces that will always be needed to protect the peace and security of an international and equal, if still very different, citizenry?

Naive may be the easy accusation of the comfortable and powerful faced with such a disturbing project as the abolition of war. Yet there may be competing naiveties here. The naivety of those who, in spite of the continuing failure to establish justice and peace by war, persist with the old prescriptions, which may be the more dangerous in the times ahead. Perhaps the naivety of the 'abolitionists', given a sufficiently sophisticated programme, may be safer and more successful in the longer term.

An extract from
The Raggy Boy[1]

PATRICK GALVIN

A year after my grandfather's death I met Mannie Goldman. Mannie lived in the Marsh, the poorest part of the city, and earned his living writing letters for people who couldn't write themselves. Halfpenny a page, envelopes free, bring your own stamp. I knocked on Mannie's door.

'Go away!'

I opened the door and fell headlong over a pile of books.

'Stupid boy! Do you realise what you've done? The entire history of the Roman Empire lies hidden in there.'

'I'm sorry, Mr Goldman. But there's no light.'

'That's your bad luck. At my age I don't need a light. Sit down.'

'Where, Mr Goldman?'

'There! Beside you. Jane Austen. Sit on her.'

I sat on Jane Austen. My first contact with creative literature. Mr Goldman lit a candle.

'Can you see now?'

'I think so, Mr Goldman.'

Mr Goldman lived in two rooms and they were both filled, from floor to ceiling, with books. They lined the walls, blocked out the windows, covered the floor and lay scattered over the bed. Apart from the bed, the only furniture Mr Goldman possessed was a chair and a table which he never used except to lay books on.

When Mr Goldman wanted to sit, he sat on the *Oxford Dictionary*, all twenty-seven volumes of it, arranged to look like a throne. And when Mr Goldman wanted something to rest his arm on, he chose his *Collected Proust*.

'It's perfectly flat,' he said, 'one of the best editions available. I strongly recommend it.'

Any money that Mr Goldman received from the letter-writing business, he spent on books. And when his cousin in America sent him five pounds every Christmas, he spent that on books. I never saw Mr Goldman eat. He fed on books.

'My wife left me. Do you know that? Couldn't stand the books. That woman was obsessed with furniture. She wanted sideboards in here. Mahogany wardrobes. Chairs, if you don't mind! Do you realise that furniture is a myth? It exists when you're there, but the moment you leave the room the furniture disappears. My wife couldn't understand that. Do you?'

'No, Mr Goldman.'

'I'm surrounded by peasants. What do you want?'

'I came to ask you about Nano Nagle, Mr Goldman.'

'Nano Nagle? You mean that female who built the South

Presentation convent? What about her? She's dead, isn't she?'

'I know that, Mr Goldman. But last night, I saw her walking up and down Margaret Street. And when I asked my father about that, he said she was in Heaven.'

'So?'

'Well, if she's in Heaven – how come she's still walking up and down Margaret Street?'

'Split personality,' said Mr Goldman. 'Have you read Freud?'

'Was he a Catholic, Mr Goldman?'

Mr Goldman almost had a stroke. 'No – he was not a flaming Catholic. But one of these days that pope of yours is going to canonise him. Ask me why. Go on – ask me why!'

'Why, Mr Goldman?'

'That's a damned good question. I'm glad you asked me. Well, before Freud came along, the Catholic Church was just about getting ready to abandon the concept of Original Sin. Then along comes Freud and hands the whole thing back to them in the form of guilt complex. Do you understand what I mean?'

I didn't. And Mr Goldman knew that I didn't. He shook his head.

'How old are you?'

'Nine.'

'Are you going to school?'

'Yes.'

'So much for education. When I was nine I was reading Dostoevsky. When I was ten I was reading Karl Marx. I under-stood him better then than I do now, but that's progress. Can you read?'

'A bit.'

'What does that mean – comics?'

'There's big books in school, Mr Goldman.'

'How big? Is there anything in them?'

'I don't know, Mr Goldman.'

'Of course you don't. Who sent you to talk to me?'

'My father.'

'Oh. I remember him. I wrote a letter for him one time. He was looking for a job. Did he get it?'

'I don't think so, Mr Goldman. He's still on the dole.'

Mr Goldman paused. 'A pity,' he said. 'Maybe next time he'll have more luck. You can go now. I've answered your question.'

'Split personality.'

'That's right. It's quite common among people with religion. Was there something else?'

'No, Mr Goldman.'

'Then off you go.'

He turned away, picked up a book and began to read. I moved towards the door and turned the handle.

'Just a minute,' he said – and lowered the book he was holding. 'I don't know why I'm doing this. I hate children. But if you want to borrow any of these books, you're welcome to do so. But ask your father first. I don't want those lunatics from the Purity League howling for my blood.'

I had never heard of the Purity League and I would ask my father. For the books fascinated me. And Mr Goldman fascinated me as he sat there on the *Oxford Dictionary*, looking like a garden gnome.

'What's going to happen to all those books when you die, Mr Goldman?'

Mr Goldman laughed. 'Die? Don't be ridiculous! But, if you must know – I've willed them all to my wife. And my one regret

174

is that I won't be around to see her face when the delivery man dumps half a million books on her doorstep.'

He laughed again and I forgot about Nano Nagle and why she was walking up and down Margaret Street when she should have been in Heaven. Maybe she didn't like Heaven, or maybe she did have a split personality as Mr Goldman had said.

I went to visit Mr Goldman every day after school and sometimes at night. He taught me to read and he taught me to write. And during the long winter evenings, when the rain danced upon those invisible windows in Mr Goldman's rooms, I sat at his feet while he read aloud from a myriad of books.

Tolstoy and Dostoevsky, Gorky and Émile Zola, Voltaire and Spinoza, Marlowe and Blake – Berkeley and Berkeley again – and for good measure the ballad history of my native city. He knew it well. His heart made room for it and it would always be there, as he was whenever I needed him.

I remember the room. The sound of his voice. The movement of his hands as he turned the pages. He read until he was tired and slept where he sat – perched high on the *Oxford Dictionary*.

When the Spanish Civil War broke out, Mr Goldman stood at the corner of Washington Street and protested against the fascists. My mother supported him, and in the evenings she painted slogans on our tenement wall, urging the natives of Cork to aid the republicans and join the International Brigades.

My father thought differently. He said that the republicans were burning the churches in Spain and he didn't want to see anything like that happening in Cork. But he refused to join the

Blueshirts, who were marching through the city wearing holy medals and appealing to the people to join them in their great crusade against the Bolsheviks.

At a huge rally in the city, Monsignor Sexton said that twenty-four Sisters of the Poor had been crucified in Barcelona, and when two men asked him for proof, they were thrown into the River Lee and had to be rescued by the Salvation Army.

The Salvation Army said that it was their Christian duty to rescue people from the River Lee and offered to make tea for everybody, if only they'd be sensible and go home. But the crowd didn't go home. They knelt in the streets and prayed for General Franco.

At the corner of Washington Street, Mr Goldman still stood and protested loudly. My mother brought him a bowl of soup from the Penny Dinner house in Hanover Street, but he refused to eat it. He said he was starving for Spain. She offered to mend a hole in his jacket, too – but he said he was quite capable of doing that himself – though he never did.

He looked weary and old, as if he'd seen it all before and there was little he could do now to prevent it happening again. I wondered where he'd grown up and about his family background. He never mentioned it.

In the evenings, I sat at his feet and listened to him read. And during the day I attended school and listened to Brother Reynolds talking about Spain. Brother Reynolds knew everything about Spain. He'd read it in the newspapers. He said that Spain was a Catholic country and the communists were out to destroy it. He said the communists were everywhere. But if they were, so was General Franco.

Franco's photograph appeared in every newspaper. His eyes peered at you out of every shop window. And his spirit haunted the classroom where Brother Reynolds was telling us that what was happening in Spain today could be happening in Ireland tomorrow.

Atrocities were being committed out there. Children were being burned alive by the Reds, and their ashes scattered on pig farms in Galicia. Priests were being hanged. Bishops were being shot through the eyes. Nuns were being raped. And when my friend Connors asked him what rape meant, he split him over the head with a metal ruler and told him to wash his mouth out with salt and then drench himself in holy water. He asked us to pray.

We should pray for General Franco. We should pray for the Moors who were fighting now to save Christianity. We should pray for the Blueshirts and join them today and be remembered forever in the Great Book of Names that was now being prepared in Heaven by Blessed Michael and his angels.

My friend Connors threw up – and others joined the Blueshirts. They danced and they marched and they wore uniforms and looked like boy scouts. But when Brother Reynolds saw them, he said they were like little angels who would one day grow up to be big angels and they then could fly off to Spain and help General Franco to kill the Reds.

He appealed for money to buy guns. He placed a collection box at the school gate and said that anyone who failed to contribute would burn in Hell for all eternity. They would be tortured by demons.

When I told my mother about Brother Reynolds, she said he was a born eejit. But Mr Goldman said he was only one of many. The country was full of them. My father said nothing, but when he saw the collection box at the school gate, on his way to Mass, he kept his hand in his pocket.

One evening as I sat with Mr Goldman, listening to him read, someone threw a brick through the window. The shattered glass cascaded across the room and Mr Goldman flung his coat over my head. We sat in the dark and waited for a second brick. But there was only one – and it was followed by a man's voice shouting, 'Dirty Jew. You murdered Christ!'

The following day, Mr Goldman returned to the corner of Washington Street. He continued to protest.

⋆⇒⚬ ⚬⇐⋆

Jewtown was a long row of red-brick corporation houses situated close to the gasworks. The houses had lain derelict for years but were now occupied by the Jews. When I asked my father about that, he said that the Jews there had come from Limerick and, before that, Romania – or some other such place. They were first persecuted there, and then in Limerick their graveyard had been desecrated by vandals. Now they had settled in Cork.

'The Lord help them,' he said.

Jewtown was bleak. But on summer days the women sat on the pavement outside their doors, knitting scarves and pullovers which they later sold around the houses in Evergreen Street and Turner's Cross. The men remained inside. And if you looked through the windows you could see them making leather belts, wallets and handbags – all decorated with twisted pieces of coloured string and beads.

My father said the Jews were poor, but Mr Egan said they were all rich. My father said he was thick.

'If they're rich, what the hell are they doing living in Jewtown!' he shouted. 'I wouldn't keep a dog in a place like that.'

178

Mr Egan said that was camouflage. You couldn't be up to the Jews; they'd have the eyes out of your head if you weren't looking.

My father turned his back on Mr Egan and refused to talk to him any more. I've been listening to that kind of nonsense from as far back as I can remember. If you're out of work, blame the Jews. If you haven't got enough to eat, blame the Jews. If the water doesn't taste right, the Jews have probably poisoned it. And if it's not the Jews, it's the bloody witches, or both. It's like living in a madhouse.'

My mother made tea. My father sat by the fire. My mother handed him a cup.

'I don't know why you take notice of an eejit like that. You know what he's like.'

'I had to take notice. The boy was listening.'

'He's listening now,' said my mother. 'Why don't you explain?'

My father looked at me. He didn't want to explain. The subject angered him, but he felt he had to say something.

'Have you been to Jewtown?' he asked.

'Yes.'

'And you've seen those people down there?'

'I have.'

'Are they any different from us?'

'I don't know.'

'Well, I'll tell you. They're not. And some of them are a damned sight worse off. They're the most persecuted people on the face of the earth, and I have to listen to rubbish like that from Egan! Is it any wonder the country is in the state that it is?'

'Drink your tea,' said my mother, 'before you have a stroke.'

My father drank his tea and almost choked swallowing it. 'I

179

told you to be careful,' my mother scolded – and patted him on the back.

'Mr Goldman is a Jew,' I said. 'Why doesn't he live in Jewtown?'

'He used to,' my mother answered. 'It was his cousin in America who found those rooms in the Marsh. And when he left, Mannie Goldman moved in. I think the cousin still pays the rent.'

'He sends him five pounds every Christmas, too.'

'The Jews try to help each other,' said my mother. 'They have to. Nobody else will look after them.'

'Did they murder Christ?' I asked.

My parents looked at me. 'Divine Jesus!' exclaimed my father. 'Who told you that?'

I remembered the night I had sat in Mr Goldman's room when someone threw a brick through the window. I told him what happened. He turned to my mother.

'Did you know about this?'

'No. But it doesn't surprise me.'

My father paused. 'It doesn't surprise me either,' he said. And lapsed into silence. Presently, he spoke.

'I can't read,' he said. 'And I can't write – but I know how Mannie Goldman must have felt. So would your grandmother. You should ask her some time.'

'You're his father,' said my mother. 'You tell him. Trying to get a word out of Lizzie Baron is like pulling teeth.'

I sing through my father.

⋙⋘

My paternal grandmother, Lizzie Baron, sat by the window of her room in Mary Street and watched the children playing handball against the side wall of Miss Mac's sweet shop directly opposite. She sat there every day now – ever since my grandfather had died and she had decided not to leave the house anymore. I went to visit her often, but she seldom spoke. She seemed content just to sit there, watching the children playing handball and waiting to be reunited with my grandfather.

'He was a big man,' she said. 'Biggest man in the world. He was not to be dead.'

She paced her words. Measured them out slowly, one at a time, and laid them down before me – a pavement to her mind.

I wanted to know about my grandfather. I wanted to know where they had met and whether it was true that she was Greek and my grandfather had rescued her from a band of marauding Turks. But she shrugged her shoulders, as if it were of no consequence, and continued to stare out of the window.

Presently she said: 'He talked to the stones. He wished to be buried in a wall. Your people did not do that. It was not right.'

'Do you want to be buried in a wall?'

'I lie with him,' she said.

I looked at the room. When my grandfather was alive, it seemed large and airy. Now it was small. The window was open, but the room smelled of old clothes and stale food. In the sink beside her, the unwashed crockery and china plates lay piled high – and on the floor near the fire my grandfather's boots lay turned on one side as if drying out after a day in the rain. Above the fire, the mantelpiece was bare. She had removed the clock that had stood there for years and now there was no time in the room and the only sound was that of the ball bouncing against the wall across the street.

In a corner of the room, my grandfather's bed stood as it had always stood – close to the wall and covered with a dark-red quilt. But she had made the bed, and my grandfather's nightshirt, neatly ironed, lay folded carefully across two pillows. It was the only task she performed daily. Everything else was unimportant. When I asked her about her past, she said that was unimportant. And when I asked her how she felt now about those who had persecuted her when she had first arrived in the city, she said she had seen worse and so had my grandfather, but she would not say where and asked me to change the subject. I changed the subject and asked her why my grandfather wanted to be buried in a wall.

'Did he like walls?'

'No,' she said. 'He did not like walls.' And left it at that.

My mother was right. Trying to get information from Lizzie Baron was like pulling teeth. I tried again.

'If he didn't like walls,' I said, 'why did he want to be buried in one?'

She turned her head, studied me for a moment and replied – 'Stones. There is truth in stones. Can you swim?'

'Swim?'

'Your grandfather could swim. He was a fine swimmer. I saw him. He rose from the water like a bird. He lay on the sand naked. He was naked in the woods. Always naked. Always beautiful. Not to be dead.'

I looked at her face. I had no idea what she was talking about. I couldn't imagine my grandfather being naked. I had never thought of him as being beautiful and I had never seen him swim.

'Why was he naked?' I asked.

She smiled. And for a moment I thought she was mocking me. But her eyes were sad, and when I looked down at her hands they were held tightly together and the knuckles glowed white from pressure and tension.

'Why?' I persisted. But she refused to answer and lowered her head.

I felt guilty then and knew that, somehow, it was wrong to question her. She was struggling for words. She didn't want to answer questions anymore. She had said enough.

'I'm sorry,' I said. 'I won't ask you again.'

She raised her head, paused for a moment, and then moved towards the bed. When she reached the bed, she knelt on the floor beside it and pulled out a tin box from beneath. Opening the box, she withdrew a number of tattered and faded photographs. She handed them to me. They were photographs of walls.

On the ground beside one wall, a group of people lay dead. The wall above them was pockmarked with bullet holes. Against another wall, two children stood facing the camera. They looked puzzled and hungry. A third wall was blank, apart from what appeared to be a list of names scratched along the side in a language I did not understand. A fourth showed a man and a woman standing beside it, holding hands. And the last photograph was of a wall covered with photographs of men, women and children.

The photographs frightened me and I wondered what they meant and why she was showing them to me now. She said nothing and just sat there on the floor watching me as I turned them over and looked at them again.

'The children,' I said. 'Who are they?'

'No questions,' she said. 'Just look.'

I looked at the one showing the man and the woman holding hands. I wanted to ask who they were, too, but I knew she wouldn't answer me.

The woman was small. Her eyes stared at the camera and out beyond it to something far off in the distance. She wore dark clothes and her long black hair hung loosely over her shoulders and down her waist. The man beside her was tall. He was wearing a pair of short trousers. His chest was bare and his feet were bare. He was looking at the woman and in his right hand he carried a revolver.

I turned to the remaining photographs, but my grandmother stretched out her hand and said: 'Give them to me now.' I gave her the photographs and she held them in her hand for a moment before replacing them in the tin box and returning the box to its place beneath the bed. Then she rose to her feet, crossed the room again and resumed her seat near the window.

I sat close beside her and together we watched the children playing in the street. We heard the sound of the ball as it bounced, backwards and forwards, against the wall of Miss Mac's sweet shop.

→⊫◎ ◎⊨←

It was one of those long blue and lazy afternoons in autumn and along the Mardyke the trees were shedding their leaves for the last time in Mr Goldman's life. He knew it would be the last time and he said so without rancour or regret.

'I grow old,' he said. 'What else is there for me to do but to die gracefully.'

'Are you a hundred?' I asked.

'Maybe two,' he replied. 'And you?'

'I'll be twelve in August.'

'You're growing old too,' he said. 'Soon now, you'll be as old as I am.'

We sat on the park bench and watched the leaves falling from the trees. They formed a glittering golden scatter along the pathway, and he said, 'You'd never think to look at them now that they were once green and springing.'

He shook his head, opened his newspaper carefully and stared at the headlines. I could tell he was old. The grey lines of his time wrinkled his forehead and the brown spots on his hands mirrored his days. He read the small print with a magnifying glass and I could almost hear his bones creak.

'They're dying in Madrid,' he said. 'It'll be over soon. Have you been to school today?'

'No.'

'Mitching again? You should go to school. You might learn something there. I can't teach you everything.'

'You've taught me a lot.'

'Maybe. But there's always something more.'

'Like what?'

'I don't know. But something.'

He folded his newspaper with extreme care and raised his head. I could see the tears in his eyes.

'The important thing,' he said – and paused. 'The important thing now is to know what's happening in the world. The Spaniards know about things like that. Would you like to go to Madrid?'

'Would you?'

'I'm too old. I was even too old when the war started. But I should have tried to go anyway instead of standing at street corners protesting. That's easy.'

'You did what you could.'

'Maybe. But it's too late now anyway. Franco will be in Madrid in no time at all.'

'My father says the war will be over then.'

'And what does your mother say?'

'She thinks there'll be an even bigger war later on.'

'She's probably right. Let's go for a walk.'

He placed the folded newspaper inside his overcoat pocket and held me by the hand. We walked towards the bandstand.

'Sometimes,' he said, 'they play some wonderful music there. It fills the air. Do you like music?'

'Yes. People come to our house every Sunday and play music all the time.'

'Of course. I'd forgotten that. It's a nice custom.'

He paused, leaned against the bandstand and said: 'You know, when I was in Spain, many years ago, I used to sit in the cafés every night and listen to the Spaniards playing the music of their lives. I don't suppose they're playing a great deal of music now.'

'Do you like the Spaniards?'

'Very much. They're a remarkable people.'

The bandstand was closed. There would be no music that day. Not until the weekend. It was not a holiday. A number of unemployed dockers were lying on the grass, enjoying the afternoon sun, and a group of children were playing rounders close to the Western Road.

'One of these days there'll be an accident there,' he said. 'It's too close to the road. Do you want to go home now?'

'I think so. I feel sad today, for some reason.'

'Me, too. Try and go to school tomorrow. Perhaps I'll see you afterwards. It's a pity about the music.'

'Yes.'

He turned away and I watched him walking slowly back towards the park bench. When he reached the bench, he sat down again and removed the folded newspaper from his overcoat pocket. He looked at the headlines, studied the small print with the aid of a magnifying glass, and wiped his eyes with a clean handkerchief. He moved on. *Viva La Quince Brigada*, old stock. *Viva La Quince Brigada*.

The 'unwilling bosom whereon it was set': Bowen's Court and the Fields of North Cork[1]

EIBHEAR WALSHE

In an essay 'Prints on the scene: Elizabeth Bowen and the landscape of childhood', in his collection entitled *The Irish Story*, Roy Foster discusses a curious episode in which Elizabeth Bowen's name was excluded from an anthology of north-Cork writing. To be more precise, her deleted name was pointedly included. In Foster's own words:

> The effort to define congruent literary geography, as suggested earlier in this book, has been a recurring preoccupation in

Irish cultural commentary – and it is not over yet. A mystifyingly crude version was produced in 1993 by the editor of the shadowy Aubane Historical Society's eccentric North Cork Anthology. The contents page includes the name of 'Elizabeth Dorothea Cole Bowen CBE' – with a line drawn through it. The editor explains laboriously that this is to show that though some people may think Elizabeth Bowen is an Irish writer, this is not the case. 'She was English ... Most of her novels are still in print due to an English demand for them.' Even more damningly, 'she was not a North Cork writer, in the sense of being a product of North Cork society, or in being interested in it or writing about it'.[2]

This attempt to deny Elizabeth Bowen her north-Cork grounding is clearly doomed to failure. Her family had been settled in Farahy for nearly 200 years by the time of her birth in 1899, and Bowen herself spent every childhood summer at Bowen's Court until her father's nervous breakdown in 1907. As an adult, Bowen divided her life between England and Farahy, and on her death in 1973 was buried next to her husband and father in the local churchyard. This identification with Ireland and particularly with north Cork and with the landscape around Farahy energised her as a writer, particularly at times of disturbance. In her last volume of memoirs, *Pictures and Conversations*, Bowen tells us: 'Am I not manifestly a writer from whom places loom large? As a reader, it is to the place-element that I react most strongly; for me, what gives fiction verisimilitude is its topography.[3] Bowen's topography in *The Last September* and *A World of Love*, and in stories like 'Summer Night' and 'The Happy Autumn Fields', is the north-Cork landscape around Bowen's Court, imaginatively transformed into a powerful, mute and devouring presence. Her imaginative debt to this landscape is made clear in *Pictures and Conversations*:

> Since I started writing, I have been welding together an inner landscape, assembled anything built at random. But if not at random, under the influence of what? ... A writer needs to have at command, and recourse to, a recognisable world, geographically consistent and having for him or her super reality.[4]

The fields and mountains around Farahy provided Bowen with this inner landscape, yet, despite biographical and textual evidence to the contrary, Bowen's place in an anthology of north-Cork writing was denied. Why? Perhaps this denial is a response to Bowen's fact-finding activities during the Second World War, when she volunteered to provide secret reports on Ireland and Irish neutrality for the British Ministry of Information. Perhaps also a residual hostility towards her class – a hostility Bowen would have understood perfectly because, in her fiction, her imagined north-Cork fields were infused with a lethal hostility.

In this essay, I want to consider the disjunction between Bowen's critical writings on the Anglo-Irish and her fictive representations of the 'Big House' in the north-Cork landscape. I agree with Roy Foster when he writes that

> When Elizabeth Bowen wrote about this part of Cork, her sense of familiar life and her love of place transcended religion, descent and political opinions ... So much of her writing (and, I suspect, much of her life) concerned an effort to establish permanence.[5]

This yearning towards a sense of permanence is at the basis of her wartime essays, but, at the same time, I would suggest that Bowen's fictive writing implicitly subverts much of her critical work. At times of violence, Bowen used her learning and her sharp critical intelligence to locate solidity, but her literary imagination was moved by a contradictory impulse to explode permanence. Bowen's underlying desire is to present a sinister threat of extinction lurking somewhere out there in the north-Cork landscape. Her fiction reveals a darker version of her anxiously utopian vision of the fields around Farahy presented in her memoirs and essays. Thus, Foster's analysis of Bowen's wartime critical writings needs a wider contextualising – the context of her wartime fictions. I agree with Foster when he writes:

> The permanence that Bowen sought, in writing about her Irish past (while the world exploded at war all around her) required an exploration of memory – the only place where, as Proust had taught, permanence resides. A recognised landscape would take her there: that sheltered Farahy landscape from where, she wrote 'personal pain evaporates, as history evaporates'.[6]

Yet this very same Farahy landscape proves murderous in *The Last September* and again in her Irish fiction written during the Second World War. Overall, her desire for the harmonious integration of the Big House within the north-Cork landscape is at odds with her fictive representations of the besieged house, cowering in the hostile fields. In Bowen's imagined fields, houses are terrorised, the light is devouring and murderous, and young men die mysteriously. As an essayist, Bowen strained towards the vision of an integrated Anglo-Irish house, at ease in the fields beneath the Ballyhoura hills. However, as a novelist, Bowen knew better.

Nowhere is Bowen's acute sense of a lone house set in a brooding landscape more strikingly represented than in her 1929 novel of the Irish War of Independence, *The Last September*. In this novel, Bowen idealised her Anglo-Irish protagonists for their courage in the face of imminent extinction at the hands of the emergent Irish revolutionaries. Sir Richard and Lady Naylor of Danielstown, the house at the centre of the novel, carry on the civilised forms of country life in the face of rebellion and insurrection, and defend their traditional feudal relationship with the native Irish. Both Naylors resent the enforced protection of the British army, and refuse to acknowledge that life in the Irish Big House is, in the indiscreet words of their nephew Laurence, 'rolling up rather'.[7] However, throughout the narrative, Bowen displaces the Anglo-Irish dread of attack and extinction away from the native Irish themselves and onto the north-Cork landscape. This is particularly evident in this description of the Big House, Danielstown, glimpsed at a distance by the protagonist, Lois:

> To the south, below them, the demesne trees of Danielstown made a dark formal square like a rug on the green country. In their heart, like a dropped pin, the grey glazed roof reflecting at the wide, light, lovely, unloving country, the unwilling bosom whereon it was set, the sky lightly glinted. Looking down it seemed to Lois they lived in a forest; spaces of lawns blotted out in the pressure and dusk of trees. She wondered they were not smothered; then wondered still more that they were not afraid. Far from here too, their isolation became apparent. The house seemed to be pressing down low in

apprehension, hiding its face, as though it had her vision of where it was. It seemed to gather its trees close in fright and amazement set.[8]

Commenting on this passage, Julian Moynahan makes the point that:

The deliberate anthropomorphism brings out the pathos of the beleaguered, beautiful lonesome tradition that the natives are struggling to be rid of. She sees the estate as a jewel; others, spying from the mountains and attacking from under the protective dusk of dense trees, see instead the chains by which jewels like Danielstown hung upon the unwilling bosom of the country.[9]

The Last September may be Bowen's elegy for the fall of the Anglo-Irish and the loss of a civilisation, but the overt conflict within the narrative arises from the mutual incomprehension between the Anglo-Irish and the visiting British military. Much of the social comedy of the novel comes from the distaste felt by Lady Naylor for her socially inferior English defenders:

I always find the great thing in England is to have plenty to say, and mercifully they are determined to find one amusing. But if one stops talking, they tell one the most extraordinary things, about their husbands, their money affairs, and their insides.[10]

Beneath Lady Nalyor's puzzled contempt for the English lies a steely determination to prevent the marriage of her niece, Lois, to the young officer, Gerald Lesworth. The threat posed by this

English youth of unknown bourgeois stock is much greater for Lady Naylor than the covert activities of the local Irish freedom fighters. Lady Naylor succeeds in breaking the engagement between her niece and the English officer, but is imaginatively implicated, to some degree, with Lesworth's subsequent murder at the hands of the local IRA. These shadowy, unnamed figures are the real threat to Danielstown, and the landscape is the visible signifier of this anonymous threat. At an early point in the novel, Lois encounters a solitary IRA man walking through her uncle's demesne late at night. This faceless Irish revolutionary is characterised by resolve, anonymity and stealth, and is a visible warning of doom for the house.

> The trench coat rustled across the path ahead, to the swing of a steady walker. She stood by the holly immovable, blotted out in her black, and there passed within reach of her hand, with the rise and fall of a stride, a resolute profile, powerful as a thought. In gratitude for its fleshliness, she felt prompted to make some contact: not to be known seemed like a doom: extinction.[11]

Lois is ignored by this unnamed, resolute profile, but the house clearly fears the lone revolutionary as a harbinger of execution.

> The crowd of trees, straining up from passive disputed earth, each sucking up and exhaling the country's essence – swallowed him finally … Below, the house waited; vast on its west side, with thin yellow lines round the downstairs shutters. It had that excluded, sad, irrelevant look outsides of houses take in the dark.[12]

In the closing moments of the novel, Bowen allows this violence to emerge with shocking force with the murder of the house:

> For in February, before those leaves had visibly budded, the death – execution, rather – of the three houses, Danielstown, Castle Trent, Mount Isabel, occurred in the same night. A fearful scarlet ate up the hard spring darkness: indeed, it seemed that an extra day, unreckoned, had come into abortive birth that these things might happen. It seemed, looking from east to west at the sky tall with scarlet, that the country itself was burning; while to the north the neck of mountains before Mount Isabel was frightfully outlined. The roads in unnatural dusk ran dark with movement, secretive or terrified; not a tree, brushed pale by wind from the flames, not a cabin pressed in despair to the bosom of the night, not a gate too starkly visible but had its place in the design of order and panic. At Danielstown, halfway up the avenue, the thin iron gate twanged (missed its latch, remained swinging aghast) as the last unlit car slid out with the executioners bald from accomplished duty. The sound of the last car widened, gave itself to the open and empty country and was demolished. Then the first wave of a silence that was to be ultimate flowed back, confident, to the steps. Above the steps, the door stood open hospitably upon a furnace.[13]

This novel represents Bowen's most sustained engagement with Ireland, but it must be remembered that few of her other novels drew on her own country for inspiration. Her novels of the 1930s, *To The North, Friends and Relations,* and her most celebrated novel, *The Death of the Heart,* all had English settings and English characters, and it is not until the Second World War that Bowen turns her fictive and critical attention back to Ireland again.

Times of violence were also times of intense creativity for Bowen. As she put it herself:

> During the war I lived, both as a civilian and as a writer, with every pore open … arguably, writers are always slightly abnormal people: certainly in so-called 'normal' times, my sense of the abnormal has been very acute. In war, this feeling of slight differentiation was suspended: I felt one with and just like, everyone else … We all lived in a state of lucid abnormality.[14]

Out of this lucid abnormality came a flood of writing about Ireland: *Bowen's Court* in 1942, *Seven Winters* in 1943, and stories like 'The Happy Autumn Fields' in 1945. In all of these Irish writings, Bowen looked homewards to north Cork as a place of stability and loyalty in an endangered and treacherous world, and her vision of Anglo-Ireland becomes her talisman, her source for imaginative power and stability in war-disordered London. However, unease continues to lurk out in the north-Cork terrain. The tensions of being Anglo-Irish at a time when Britain was at war while Ireland remained neutral accentuated Bowen's ambivalent attitude towards Ireland. In the words of the critic, Heather Bryant Jordan: 'Unable to abandon her colonial training, Bowen found herself in the midst of a battle with institutions that echoed her own skirmishes with herself.'[15] These skirmishes meant that, even in her most celebratory work, her childhood memoir, *Seven Winters*, she still writes of her birth in the following terms:

So by having been born where I had been born in a month in which that house did not exist, I felt that I had intruded on some no-place'.[16]

To compensate, Bowen's critical writings of the early 1940s show her at her most determinedly optimistic. The best example of this kind of writing comes with her 1942 essay 'The Big House', first published by her friend and lover, Seán Ó Faoláin, in his pluralist journal, *The Bell*. Ó Faoláin founded this magazine to counterbalance the oppressive cultural insularity and xenophobia of Ireland in the 1930s and 1940s, and he invited Bowen to speak up, as it were, for the marginalised and antagonistic Anglo-Irish of post-independence Ireland. Bowen seized this opportunity to argue for a valid place for the Anglo-Irish in contemporary Ireland. Thus, her essay is a plea for assimilation, a utopian vision of a harmonious relationship between house and landscape. Her tone throughout the piece is jaunty:

The loneliness of my house, as of many others, is more an effect than a reality ... When I visit other big houses I am struck by some quality that they all have – not so much isolation as mystery ... they were planned for spacious living – for hospitality above all.[17]

Yet, despite her need to create a place for the Big House in twentieth-century Ireland, her particular sense of the strangeness of the Big House within the countryside inevitably breaks through in this essay.

The Big House people were handicapped, shadowed and to

an extent queered by their pride, by their indignation at their decline and by their divorce from the countryside in whose heart their struggle was carried out.[18]

She concludes her essay with a call for political and cultural accommodation between Big House and surrounding towns and villages:

> The Big House has much to learn – and it must learn if it is to survive at all. But it also has much to give. From inside many big houses (and these will be the survivors) barriers are being impatiently attacked. But it must be seen that a barrier has two sides.[19]

At the same time, Bowen's most ambitious wartime writing on Ireland was a history of her family home, *Bowen's Court*, published in 1942. In this family chronicle, she proudly presents successive Bowen patriarchs and landowners as members of a powerful dynasty, and addresses the difficult question of attempted harmonisation between house and surrounding lands. However, blankness and non-being threatened to descend on the Big House, and the threat of violence is never quite exorcised:

> Inside and about the house and in the demesne woods you feel transfixed by the surrounding emptiness; it gives depth to the silence, quality to the light. The land around Bowen's Court, even under its windows, has an unhumanised air the house does nothing to change. Here are, even, no natural features, view or valley to which the house may be felt to relate itself. It has set, simply, its pattern of trees and avenues on the virgin, anonymous countryside.[20]

As Hermione Lee writes of *Bowen's Court*:

> It is the story of what happens to a minority when they lose
> the confidence, which enabled them to build, as they did in
> the eighteenth century. It describes a 'big' impersonal, digni-
> fied concept of living – 'traditional sanctity and loveliness'
> – going into retreat. So *Bowen's Court* is intimately related
> to Bowen's fiction, all of which is concerned with how to live
> in a world where rootedness, acquisitions, permanence – the
> Burkean ' goods' – are at risk, and where a decorous idea of
> behaviour has degenerated into the dire period of Personal
> Life.[21]

In her descriptions of the land surrounding the north-Cork towns
of Doneraile and Mallow, the risky business of attempting to
locate permanence is to the forefront of her mind. For example,
she describes Edmund Spenser's time in Ireland in terms that
have little or no basis in historical fact, and show some slight
sense of Spenser's own writings on Ireland. Rather, she reflects
her own interaction with the Irish landscape:

> He liked little in Ireland: his position was sinister and des-
> olate … his castle, Kilcolman, lies two miles north-west of
> Doneraile, on an exposed plateau under the Ballyhouras; the
> marsh where gulls breed was once his smiling lake – but he
> never cared for its smile. Kilcolman keep, a torn-open ruin,
> still stands; winds race round it at every time of year. The
> view is of Ireland at its most intimidating – the marsh, the
> heartless mountains with their occasional black frown. The
> landscape fulfilled, for Spenser, its conveyed threat; the castle

was burnt by the Irish in his absence, and one of his sons, an infant, died in the fire.[22]

In contrast, her 1949 novel, *The Heat of the Day*, has a long section set in Ireland, and in this fictionalised version of the Irish Big House, she allows a sense of untroubled patriotic love between house and land to predominate. This is of a piece with Bowen's wartime sense of Anglo-Ireland as a loyal, stable place, and the Anglo-Irish home becomes symbolically implicated with eventual Allied victory. In the novel, Stella Rodney, the protagonist, visits Mount Morris, the house inherited by her soldier son. During her stay in Ireland, Stella comes to see this Irish Big House as an oasis of feudal certainty, and this certainty is contrasted unfavourably with the suffocating, traitorous suburban villas of the English Home Counties. Mount Morris is viewed by Stella in terms that contrast Lois' troubled vision of Danielstown:

> The river traced the boundary of the lands: at the Mount Morris side, it has a margin of water-meadow into which the demesne woods, dark at their base with laurels, ran down in a series of promontories. This valley cleavage into a distance seemed like an offering to the front window: in return the house devoted the whole muted fervour of its being to a long gaze. Elsewhere rising woods or swelling uplands closed Mount Morris in.[23]

While in Ireland, Stella discovers that her lover is a spy and a traitor, and she returns to London intent on confronting him. In addition, Mount Morris is the place where Stella first hears of Allied victories in north Africa, the turning point of the war. So, it seems as if Anglo-Ireland has been transmuted into a loyal, safe and trustworthy terrain by the experience of the Second World War.

However, to unsettle this possibility, I want to conclude this essay by considering one of Bowen's other wartime writings on Ireland – her story 'The Happy Autumn Fields' – and I want to suggest that in this story, the murderous fields around Farahy still hold threat. This 1945 short story, published in the collection, *The Demon Lover and Other Stories* seems, at first glance, to be at one with *The Heat of the Day*, an idealised vision of Anglo-Ireland from the perspective of Blitz London. Instead, I want to argue that the story can be read as a reprise of *The Last September*. 'The Happy Autumn Fields' centres on the hallucinations of the protagonist, Mary, slumbering in a damaged house in war-torn London. Mary is in mortal danger while she remains in the crumbling house, but she refuses to leave, addicted to her daydreams of a Victorian landlord and his family in an autumnal rural landscape. Throughout the story, a disparity is established between diminished, un-heroic wartime London and the idyllic past of Anglo-Ireland. As Mary complains:

> We only know inconvenience now, not sorrow. Everything pulverises so easily now because it is rot-dry; one can only wonder that it makes so much noise. The source, the sap must have dried up, or the pulse must have stopped, before you and I were conceived. So much flowed through people; so little flows through us. All we can do is imitate love or sorrow.[24]

Mary dreams of this unnamed landscape, the prosperous autumn fields of a country house in September – another last September.

In these fields, the Victorian patriarch walks the land with his numerous sons and daughters on the day his older sons return to boarding school. Mary imagines herself into the mind of Sarah, one of the many daughters of the landlord, possessively engrossed with her twin sister, Henrietta. The mood of these autumn fields, as seen through Sarah's eyes, is elegiac:

> She recognised the colour of valediction, tasted sweet sadness, while from the cottage inside the screen of trees wood-smoke rose melting pungent and blue.[25]

Although the Big House is never actually identified as Ireland, Bowen herself dubbed this landscape of her wartime Irish fictions 'unshakeably county Cork'.[26] As in *The Last September*, these young Anglo-Irish women, Sarah and Henrietta, catch an unexpected glimpse of their home from a distance, and the vulnerability of the Big House becomes immediately apparent:

> The shorn uplands seemed to float on the distance, which extended dazzling to tiny blue glassy hills. There was no end to the afternoon, whose light went on ripening now they had scythed the corn … Only screens of trees intersected and knolls made islands in the vast fields. The mansion and the home farm had sunk forever below them in the expanse of woods, so that hardly a ripple showed where the girls dwelled.[27]

To some degree, this is a ghost story, or at least a story about the mysterious death of a young man alone in these autumn fields. In the story, Mary dreams herself into Sarah's psyche, and shares her terror and jealousy at the arrival of the young man, Eugene, who has come to court and marry Henrietta. Eugene's untimely death, like that of Gerard Lesworth, prevents an unsuitable marriage and, again, is implicitly connected with sinister aspects of the north-Cork landscape. Here, Bowen uses the menacing silent presence of the rooks to suggest imminent extinction.

> Behind them, rooks that had risen and circled, sun striking blue from their blue black wings, plane one by one to the earth and peck again.[28]

> In the inevitable silence rooks on the return from the fields could be heard streaming over the house; their sounds filled the sky and even the room, and it appeared so useless to ring the bell that Henrietta stayed quivering by Mamma's chair.[29]

The story ends with the obliteration of the interloping young suitor by the landscape. Again, the fields around Farahy manage to accomplish their silent, murderous purpose:

> Fitzgeorge refers, in a letter to Robert written in his old age, to some friend of their youth who was thrown from his horse and killed, riding back after a visit to their home. The young man, whose name doesn't appear, was alone; and the evening, which was in autumn, was fine though late. Fitzgeorge wonders, and says he will always wonder, what made the horse shy in those empty fields.[30]

Characters

JOHN BANVILLE

I shall begin with a couple of quotations. Here are the closing
stanzas of Wallace Stevens' great poem, 'Credences of Summer':

> The personae of summer play the characters
> Of an inhuman author, who meditates
> With the gold bugs, in blue meadows, late at night.
> He does not hear his characters talk. He sees
> Them mottled, in the moodiest costumes,
>
> Of blue and yellow, sky and sun, belted
> And knotted, sashed and seamed, half pales of red,
> Half pales of green, appropriate habit for
> The huge decorum, the manner of the time,
> Part of the mottled mood of summer's whole,

> In which the characters speak because they want
> To speak, the fat, the roseate characters,
> Free, for a moment, from malice and sudden cry,
> Complete in a completed scene, speaking
> Their parts as in a youthful happiness.

And here, in all modesty, I assure you, is a paragraph from the final pages of my novel *Ghosts*. The narrator has been considering a painting by one Jean Vaublin, an invented artist – invented by me – who is not entirely dissimilar to the great Jean Antoine Watteau.

> What happens does not matter; the moment is all. This is the golden world. The painter has gathered his little group and set them down in this wind-tossed glade, in this delicate, artificial light, and painted them as angels and as clowns. It is a world where nothing is lost, where all is accounted for while yet the mystery of things is preserved; a world where they may live, however briefly, however tenuously, in the failing evening of the self, solitary and at the same time together somehow here in this place, dying as they may be and yet fixed forever in a luminous, unending instant.

Who and what are a novelist's characters? What are they to him, and what are they for him? Or, stepping down from the grand generalities so as to preserve my assumed state of modesty, let me rather ask, who and what are *my* characters, and what are they to *me*, what are they for *me*? I distrust authors who claim that at some point or other in the course of a novel their characters 'developed a life of their own' and 'took over the story'. I always assume that such authors are either liars or fools. In the particular lunatic asylum wherein we novelists work, our little manufactured madmen are never allowed to wrest the pen out of our hands and assume command.

However, we keepers of the padded cells are not entirely free, either.

When I was a young man, beginning to publish fiction, I believed that I was wholly in control of what I wrote. To Beckett's famous question, which was famously taken up by Michel Foucault, 'What does it matter who speaks?', the resounding answer for me was, 'It matters everything.' In my novel *Kepler*, for instance, published in 1981, I devised a fiendishly complicated work-scheme based on Kepler's theory of the five perfect solids – don't worry, I'm not going to attempt to expound that theory here – whereby the characters were forced to move and congregate according to a strict formula of my making. At the time I was much taken with numerology, and tried to follow artists such as Béla Bartok, who frequently composed according to the rule of golden section, and imposed forms on his works that sometimes involved counting the notes in order to make the parts accord with esoteric rules that were more magical than mathematical.

Then something happened. In the mid-1980s I broke with my own rules of engagement, and began to work in a far more instinctive way than I had heretofore. I am not sure what caused this shift, although I do remember the precise moment when it occurred, or at least I remember the precise moment when I noticed that it had occurred. My parents had died, and I suspect I was in deep, subconscious mourning for them, and in *Mefisto*, the novel I was writing at the time – this was the mid-1980s – I arrived at a section in which the narrator, wandering erratically in the wake of Goethe's Faust, paid a visit to a priestess of the Eternal Motherhood. Suddenly, I realised that I did not know what I was doing. That is to say, I was writing in a new way, unrestricted by any rational plan. Obviously, in describing my narrator's encounter with this strange, unreal, monumental Woman, I was in some way writing about my mother, who in death had become strange, and unreal, and monumental. It was a revelatory experience, and after it, I knew, nothing for me – for my writing, I mean – would ever be the same again.

Both Kafka and Beckett had similar experiences – perhaps all artists have such moments of revelation, of clarification. For Kafka, the long night from evening to dawn during which, in a white heat of composition, he wrote in its entirety the story 'The Judgement', was the occasion of his coming-of-age as an artist. Beckett's transformative insight, fragmentarily described in *Krapp's Last Tape*, came to him on Dún Laoghaire pier one stormy night at the end of the war – in fact, as Beckett told his biographer, it was not at Dún Laoghaire but in his mother's room that he received his 'revelation' – when he at last began 'to write the things I feel'. As against Joyce's method of 'always *adding* … I realised that my own way was in impoverishment, in lack of knowledge and in taking away, in subtracting rather than adding.'

What I had found – again, in my humble fashion – was a new way, for me, of presenting human experience in fictional form. The thing to do, I saw, was to move away from the realism of novels such as *Kepler* and its predecessor, *Doctor Copernicus*, and into a new realm in which I would think less and dream more – I would subtract and add – and in which my characters would have at least a certain autonomy.

Yet what does it mean to say that a 'character' will have

'autonomy'? The marionettes who populate my novels are all aspects of me, necessarily, since I am the only raw material that I have, that is, since I am the only human being I know from the inside, as it were – though what 'knowing' means in this context is a knotty philosophical question we shall not try to unravel here. My fictional characters are like the figures I encounter in my dreams, all generated out of my subconscious mind. They take the forms of others, of loved ones and strangers, friends and relations, objects of desire and harbingers of terror, but in the end they are *me*, the fragments of my self that has been temporarily disassembled by the mysterious agency of sleep.

To write fiction is to be made myriad. There is a theory in physics, the 'many worlds syndrome', which posits that reality is at every instant splitting into billions upon billions of alternatives of itself, other worlds in which each singular probability becomes a certainty. In our small and all too finite way, we novelists present ourselves with other realities in which to live out other lives. The languishing protagonist of Huysmans' *À rebours* recommended that we should let our servants do our living for us; I can have my characters do that, and much more colourfully.

I recognise the solipsism implicit in my version of what the novelist, Stevens' 'inhuman author', does. The novel is regarded as the most democratic, the most demotic, of the art forms. Henry James deplored George Eliot's *Middlemarch* for the 'loose, baggy monster' he judged it to be, yet there are many critics, and many readers, who prize the novel form precisely for its accommodating looseness, its glorious bagginess, in which the 'roseate characters' will have room to wander at will.

People insist on believing in the reality of fictional characters. Don Quixote, Emma Bovary, Leopold Bloom can seem more vividly real to us than the person sleeping in bed beside us while we sit turning the pages and biting our nails in suspense as poor Anna Karenina walks towards the railway line. The pact the reader makes with the fictional text is a fascinating one. No matter how hard one presses upon the reader's credulity and willingness to suspend disbelief, the contract holds: Lemuel Gulliver, however improbably pinned to the sand by a multitude of tiny people or quizzed by talking horses, is for us alive in one of the multiple worlds of fiction.

How is this magic trick brought off? By the power of the imagination, working in its dreamlike fashion. The imagination, that 'inhuman author', makes worlds and populates them. It is a kind of transcendent playing. Our little, lifelike figures are made, in Auden's phrase, 'out of Eros and of dust'. Who on earth are they? And are they on earth? They are real, and yet how can they be? But if unreal, what a clamour they make.

... the characters speak because they want
To speak ...

Notes & References

Three Unjustly Uncelebrated Local-government Cases
David Gwynn Morgan
(pages 33–48)

1 'The Swans' was a popular annual theatrical revue in Cork.

2 Goodman, A., *Tell Them I'm on My Way* (London, Chapmans, 1993).

3 Kelly, J. 'Administrative Discretion and the Courts', *Irish Jurist* (1966), (New Series, vol. 1), pp. 209–10.

4 Kelly, J. 'Judicial Review of Administrative Action: New Irish Trends', *Irish Jurist*, (New Series, vol. 6), (1971), p. 40. The four subsequent Irish decisions referred to were: *Listowel UDC vs. McDonagh* [1968] IR 312; *Central Dublin Development Association vs. Attorney-General* (1975) 109 ILTR 69; *Kiely vs. Minister for Social Welfare* [1971] IR 21; *East Donegal Co-Operatives Ltd. vs. Attorney-General* [1970] IR 317.

5 The inherent unlikeliness of this reminds one of a couple of remarks that curiously echo each other: in Britain, Philip Larkin remarked sarcastically, there was no extramarital intercourse before the 1960s. Similarly, an Irish bishop remarked that there was no intercourse before *The Late Late Show*.

6 [1941] Ir. Jur. Rep., pp. 81–3.

7 The first lectures on administrative law in Irish universities were given as follows: TCD (1946, FC King); UCD (early 1950s, P. McGilligan); UCG (1975, J.M.G. Sweeney); UCC (1978, D. Gwynn Morgan); QUB (1953). The earliest books were: Stout, *Administrative Law in Ireland* (Dublin, IPA, 1987); Hogan and Morgan, *Irish Administrative Law* (London, Sweet and Maxwell, 1st edn., 1987).

211

8   de Smith, S.A., *Judicial Review of Administrative Action* (London, Stevens & Sons, 1959).

9   Maitland, F.W., *The Constitutional History of England* (Cambridge, CUP, 1963 reprint), p. 505.

10 *Political Studies* (1963), vol. 11 (3) pp. 272–86.

11 Hogan G. and Gwynn Morgan, D., *Administrative Law in Ireland* (London, Sweet and Maxwell, 4th edn., forthcoming).

12 Figures from Kenny, L. *From Ballot Box to Council Chamber* (Dublin, IPA, 1999), p. 20.

Gerald Yael Goldberg
Dermot Keogh & Damien O'Mahony
(pages 49–67)

1   By kind permission of the journalists involved, this essay contains extracts from interviews with Gerald Goldberg conducted by Evelyn Ring, Liam Heylin, Michael Carr and Des O'Sullivan.

2   *The United Irishman*, 16 September 1899.

Notes on the Early History of Cork Jewry
Cormac Ó Gráda
(pages 73–93)

1   This essay draws on an ongoing monograph about the economic and demographic history of Irish Jewry. I am extremely grateful to Louis Marcus and to Andy Bielenberg for making me rethink what I wrote in an earlier draft. All remaining errors are my own.

2   See Goldberg, 1945; Hyman, 1972, ch. xxiv; Marcus, 1986, 2001. This essay describes some features of the community's economic and demographic history in the early decades.

3   Carol Weinstock, interview with David Birkhan, July 1987 in National Library of Ireland, Acc. 5734 (unsorted). This story may have its origin in the saga of the *Hispania*, which was forced to spend some weeks in Cork for repairs in 1895. The male Russian-Jewish passengers on board were billeted

in the houses of Cork co-religionists, while the women and children, who remained on board, were visited and cared for daily. A.H. Goldfoot, one of the leaders of the community, footed the grocery bills. A service was held on board the *Hispania* before its departure to America (*JC*, 7 June 1895).

4   Lentin 2001; Harris, 2001, p. 1; Marcus, 2001, p. 266; Goldberg 1982; Price 2002, p. 30.

5   Cesarani, David, 1996, pp. 251–2.

6   Hyman, p. 218–24.

7   Carol Weinstock, interview with Larry Elyan, July 1987 in National Library of Ireland, Acc. 5734.

8   The proportion of households living in Hibernian Buildings probably declined over time. Seven of the thirty-nine couples in the 1911 database described below were living in Hibernian Buildings.

9   Carol Weinstock, interview with Esther Hesselberg, National Library of Ireland, Acc, 5734. Louis Marcus remembers talk of an elderly eccentric known as *der alte* Levi.

10 Interview with Larry Elyan, 1972 (Oral History Department, Institute of Contemporary Jewry, Hebrew University of Jerusalem). The *sefer torah* is a sacred parchment scroll on which portions of the old testament have been written by hand. It is kept in the ark in the synagogue. See also Hyman, 1972, p. 219.

11 Marcus, 1986, p. 111.

12 National Archives of Ireland, CSORP 1888/15,507.

13 *The Times*, 15 March 1888.

14 Hyman, 1972, p. 219.

15 Zborowksi and Herzog, 1995, pp. 152, 156.

16 Morawska, 1996, p. 16.

17 As in Dublin, there is evidence of within-street clustering of Jewish families. Thus, in Appendix 1 half of the Jewish-occupied houses in Hibernian Buildings were numbered between 79 and 93. Jewish households also lived in numbers 30, 32 and 34.

18 *Jewish Chronicle*, 4 January 1896, 14 August 1896

19 Jessie Bloom (née Spiro), 'Dublin notes', unpublished typescript dated 1953, deposited in the Jacob Rader Marcus Center of the American Jewish Archives, Cincinnati. I have standardised the punctuation.

20 Bloom 1952, p. 30; see also Keogh, 1998, p. 16). In Cork, the pedlars were known as 'tallymen' by the Christians they dealt with. The Scottish drapers so common in nineteenth-century England were also often called 'tallymen'. See 'Memoir' by Esther Hesselberg in National Library of Ireland, Acc. 5734, undated.

21 The Jewish occupations represented in our 1911 Cork database are as follows:

2 clergymen
4 pedlars
4 commercial travellers
9 drapers
2 financiers/moneylenders
1 master capmaker
1 jeweller
1 marine dealer
1 commission agent
1 shopkeeper
1 general dealer
1 glazier
1 milk vendor
1 newsagent/stationer
1 photo enlarger
1 picture frame seller
1 travelling musician

22 *Jewish Chronicle*, 5 January 1894. The *Jewish Chronicle* often featured the Goldfoots. On 22 May 1891 it reported that Mr and Mrs Goldfoot made a presentation to the synagogue and ran a party for the entire community in the school room to mark their son's *bar mitzvah*. It also reported the achievement of Goldfoot's daughter 'at the examination of Art and Science, recently held in Cork': 'Miss Jenny Goldfoot passed in the following subjects: Freehand Drawing, Advanced Stage; Drawing in Life and Shade, Elementary Stage; Model Drawing, Elementary Stage': *Jewish Chronicle*, 24 September 1897.

23 Interview with Larry Elyan, loc. cit.

24 Perlman, 1997.

Bibliography

Bloom, J., 'The old days in Dublin: some girlhood recollections of the 1890s', *Commentary*, July 1952, pp. 21–32.

Cesarani, D., 'The myth of origins: ethnic memory and the experience of emigration', in A. Newman and S. W. Massil (eds.), *Patterns of Migration 1850–1914* (London, Jewish Historical Society of England, 1996), pp. 247–54.

Goldberg, G. Y., 'Note on the Jewish community in Cork', in B. Shillman, *A Short History of the Jews in Ireland* (Dublin, Eason, 1945), pp. 138–42.

Goldberg, G. Y., 'Ireland is the only country ... Joyce and the Jewish dimension', in M.P. Hederman and R. Kearney (eds.), *The Crane Bag Book of Irish Studies*, vol. 2, 1982–85 (London, Colin Smythe, 1982), pp. 5–12.

Harfield, E., *A Commercial Directory of the Jews of the United Kingdom* (London, 1983).

Harris, N., *Dublin's Little Jerusalem* (Dublin, A. & A. Farmar, 2001).

Hyman, L., *The Jews in Ireland from Earliest Times to 1910* (Dublin, Irish Academic Press, 1972).

Keogh, D., *Jews in Twentieth-century Ireland: Refugees, Anti-Semitism and the Holocaust* (Cork, Cork University Press, 1988).

Lentin, R., 'Ireland's other diaspora: Jewish–Irish within, Irish–Jewish without', *Golem: European Jewish Magazine*, vol. 3, no. 6 (2001).

Marcus, D., *A Land Not Theirs* (New York, Bantam Press, 1986).

Marcus, D., *Oughtobiography: Leaves from the Diary of a Hyphenated Jew* (Dublin, Gill & Macmillan, 2001).

Morawska, E., *Insecure Prosperity: Small-town Jewry in Industrial America 1890–1940* (Princeton, Princeton University Press, 1996).

Perlmann, J., 'Russian Jewish literacy in 1897: a reanalysis of census data', in S. della Pergola and J. Even (eds.), *Papers in Jewish Demography 1993 in Memory of U.O. Schmeltz* (Jerusalem, Avraham Harman Institute of Contemporary Jewry, 1997), pp. 123–36.

Price, S., *Somewhere to Hang my Hat* (Dublin, New Island Books, 2003).

Zborowski, M. and Herzog, E., *Life is With People: The Culture of the Shtetl* (New York, Schocken, 1995; first published in 1952).

'Making *Aliya*': Irish Jews, the Irish State and Israel
Dermot Keogh
(pages 105–40)

1   This article is based largely on a survey of the archives of the Department of Foreign Affairs and the Department of the Taoiseach; Archbishop John Charles McQuaid's papers in the Dublin Archdiocesan Archives; and interviews conducted in Israel in June 2001. Dr Paula Wylie, a former doctoral student working under my direction, completed a case study on Ireland's recognition of Israel as part of her work. I am very grateful to her for having supplied me with a range of documents that

she discovered on Ireland and Israel during the Suez Crisis. She generously allowed me to publish them as part of this study.

2 For background, see Laqueur, W., *A History of Zionism* (New York, Holt, Rinehart and Winston, 1972).

3 Reich, B. and Goldberg, D.H., *Political Dictionary of Israel* (Lanham, Maryland and London, Scarecrow Press, 2000); see entries for *Aliya* and Zionism, p. 11 and p. 429.

4 Keogh, D., *Jews in Twentieth-Century Ireland: Refugees, Anti-Semitism and the Holocaust* (Cork, Cork University Press, 1998), chapter 2.

5 Reich and Goldberg, *Political Dictionary of Israel*; see entry for *Aliya*, p. 11.

6 For population statistics, see Keogh, *Jews in Twentieth-Century Ireland*, pp. 9–11; Censuses of Population, Republic of Ireland.

7 Census of Ireland, Province of Ulster, 1891 and 1911; Census of Population of Northern Ireland, 1937; data kindly supplied by Dr Caroline Windrum.

8 Censuses of Northern Ireland; data kindly supplied by Dr Caroline Windrum.

9 Gilbert, J.Z., 'Zionism in Ireland', *Encyclopedia of Zionism and Israel* (New York, McGraw-Hill, 1971), p. 552.

10 Ibid.

11 Ibid.

12 Ibid.

13 Ibid.

14 Keogh, *Jews in Twentieth-Century Ireland*, pp. 67–8, 91, 231–2.

15 Ibid., pp. 78–82, 88, 124, 162.

16 Briscoe, R. (with Hatch, A.), *For the Life of Me* (New York, Little Brown and Company, 1958), pp. 264–5.

17 Yahil, L., *The Holocaust: The Fate of European Jewry* (Oxford and New York, Oxford University Press, 1991), pp. 188–9.

18 For a study of his early life, see Katz, S., *Lone Wolf: A Biography of Vladimir (Ze'en) Jabotinsky* (New Jersey, Barricade, 1996), 2 vols.

19 Yahil, *The Holocaust*, p. 188.

20 Ibid.

21 Wasserstein, B., *Britain and the Jews of Europe 1939–1945* (Oxford and New York, Oxford University Press, 1988), p. 12.

22 Kennedy, B., *Ireland and the League of Nations: International Relations, Diplomacy and Politics* (Dublin, Irish Academic Press, 1996), p. 254.

23 *Zion News*, 20 December 1937, p. 5.

24 Briscoe, *For the Life of Me*, p. 267 ff.

25   Ibid., pp. 264–5.

26   *Irish Press*, 12 December 1938. The members of the committee, under the chairmanship of Dr Abrahamson, were Robert Briscoe, Dr Baker and H. Good; see D/FA, 105/51, NAI.

27   Keogh, *Jews in Twentieth-Century Ireland*, p. 297.

28   Briscoe, *For the Life of Me*, p. 267 ff.

29   Boland Memorandum, 9 February 1948, D/FA, 305/62/1, NAI.

30   Mordecai Naor, *The Twentieth Century in Eretz Israel* (Bnei Brak, Israel: Steinmatzky, 1998), pp. 256–94.

31   MacBride telegram and reply, Embassy to the Holy See [Box 2], 14/68/1, D/FA, NAI.

32   Keogh, D., 'The Role of the Catholic Church in the Republic of Ireland 1922–1995', in *Building Trust in Ireland* (Belfast, Blackstaff Press, 1996).

33   Various resolutions from county councils and vocational education committees in D/FA 305/62/1, NAI.

34   Jakobovits, I., *Journal of a Rabbi* (London, W.H. Allen, 1967), p. 56.

35   Ibid., p. 126.

36   McQuaid to Jakobovits, 26 May 1949, D/FA 305/62/1, NAI; the letter on file is typed but signed by the archbishop himself. The words 'the international status of Jerusalem' are written in his own hand. Why would a letter of this kind be sent in draft form to Iveagh House? Is it possible that Ambassador Walshe had privately advised the archbishop on the content of the reply to Rabbi Jakobovits?

37   Ibid.

38   Ibid.

39   Ibid.

40   Ibid. The archbishop ended: 'May I thank you again for the ready courtesy with which you have graciously accepted my suggestions in the present crisis, and may I assure you of my constant goodwill in assisting you to find a just and sympathetic solution to the difficulties of the situation.'

41   Jakobovits, *Journal of a Rabbi*, p. 126.

42   Department of Foreign Affairs File, box 1, Holy Land Folder, John Charles McQuaid Papers, Dublin Archdiocesan Archives. DDA McQuaid papers, AB8/B/XVIII.

43   Ibid.

44   Ibid.

45   Ibid.

46   Ibid.

47   Ibid.

48   Ibid.

49   Ibid.

50   Dáil Éireann debates, vol. 117, cols. 866–7, 13 July 1949.

51   MacBride to Walshe, 22 August 1949, D/FA 305/62/1, NAI.

52   Memorandum by T.J.H., Department of External Affairs, 11 November 1952, D/FA, 305/62/1, NAI.

53   Ibid.

54   Ibid.

55   Ibid.

56   Ibid.

57   Embassy to the Holy See [box 2], 14/68/1, D/FA, NAI.

58   Ibid.

59   Ibid.

60   Ibid.

61   Ibid.

62   Damien Cole, Middle East Section, Department of Foreign Affairs to me, 8 February 1996.

63   Israel and the Holy See made a joint declaration on 29 June 1992 announcing the establishment of a permanent bilateral working commission aimed at initiating diplomatic relations. The 'fundamental agreement' between Israel and the Holy See was signed on 29 December 1993; Minerbi, S.I., 'The Vatican and Israel', in Kent, P. and Pollard, J. (eds), *Papal Diplomacy in the Modern Age* (Westport and London, Prager, 1994), p. 189.

64   Steinberg to Seán Murphy, Secretary, Department of External Affairs, 31 March 1956, D/FA 319/25/9, NAI. (This and subsequent references on this issue were kindly supplied to me by Dr Paula Wylie.)

65   Jakobovits to Seán Murphy, Secretary, Department of External Affairs, 26 March 1956, D/FA 319/25/9, NAI.

66   Dublin to Biggar, London Embassy, 14 September 1956, D/FA 319/25/9, NAI.

67   Murphy to Secretary, Department of Finance, 7 September 1956, D/FA 319/25/9, NAI.

68   Departmental minutes by Woods, 12 July 1956, D/FA 319/25/9, NAI.

69   Murphy to Secretary, Department of Finance, 7 September 1956, D/FA 319/25/9, NAI.

70   I am grateful to Professor David Birkhahn for writing this piece for this volume.

'Dabru Emet': Its Significance for
Jewish–Christian Dialogue
Rabbi David Rosen
(pages 145-55)

1   An address given at the twentieth-anniversary celebration of the Dutch Council of Christians and Jews (OJEC) at Tilburg, the Netherlands, 6 November 2001.

2   See http://www.jcrelations.net

3   www.yucs.org/~cypess/rav/

4   'Confrontation', published in *Tradition – A Journal of Orthodox Jewish Thought*, vol. 6 (2) (1964).

5   *Face to Face – an Interreligious Bulletin*, vol. 2 (winter/spring 1977).

6   *The Great Hatred*, Samuel, M. (New York, Knopf, A.A, 1940), pp. 36, 56, 127–8, 142.

7   Bemporad, J. (Rabbi), *Current Dialogue*, vol. 41 (July 2003), published by the WCC.

8   See Guttman, J., *Die Philosophie des Judentums* (Munich, Ernst Reinhardt, 1933).

9   Seder Olam Rabbah 33–35; Sefer Hashimush 15–17; see Falk, H., 'Rabbi Jacob Emden's Views on Christianity', *Journal of Ecumenical Studies*, vol. 19, no. 1 (winter 1982).

10 Address to the Jewish Community, Mainz, Germany, 17 November 1980, reprinted in Fisher, E. J. and Klenicki, L. (eds.), *Spiritual Pilgrimage*, Pope John Paul II's texts on Jews and Judaism (New York, Crossroad, 1995), p. 13.

From *Shoa* to *Shalom*: The Case for Abolishing War
in the Twenty-first Century
Enda McDonagh
(pages 157–70)

1   Hogan, L. and Fitzgerald, B. (eds.), *Between Poetry and Politics: Essays in Honour of Enda McDonagh* (Dublin, Columba, 2003).

An extract from *The Raggy Boy*
Patrick Galvin
(pages 171–87)

1 These extracts from *The Raggy Boy Trilogy* (Dublin, New Island, 2002) have been reproduced with the kind permission of Patrick Galvin and New Island.

The 'unwilling bosom whereon it was set': Bowen's Court and the Fields of North Cork
Eibhear Walshe
(pages 189–204)

1 This essay was originally published as 'Bowen and the Terrain of North Cork' in *Estudios Irlandeses*, 2005 (University of Barcelona), pp. 140–77.

2 Foster, R., *The Irish Story* (London, Penguin, 2001), p. 148.

3 Bowen, E., *Pictures and Conversations* (London, Allen Lane, 1975), p. 34.

4 Ibid. p. 36.

5 Foster, R., op. cit. p. 21.

6 In an essay entitled, 'The Landscape of Childhood', op. cit. p. 152.

7 Bowen, E., *The Last September* (London, Penguin, 1987), p. 25.

8 Ibid. p. 66.

9 Moynahan, J., *Anglo-Irish* (Princeton, Princeton University Press, 1995), p. 242

10 Bowen, E., *The Last September*, op. cit. p. 134.

11 Ibid. p. 134.

12 Ibid.

13 Ibid. p. 206.

14 Bowen, E., *The Demon Lover and Other Stories* (London, Cape, 1947), p. 190.

15 Jordan, Heather Bryant, *How Will the Heart Endure* (Ann Arbor: The University of Michigan, 1992), p. 100.

16 Bowen, E., *Seven Winters* (London, Longmans, 1943), p. 7.

17 Walshe, E. (ed.), *Elizabeth Bowen Remembered* (Dublin, Four Courts, 1999), p. 61.

18 Ibid. p. 63.

19   Ibid. p. 65.
20   Bowen, E., *Bowen's Court* (Cork, The Collins Press, 1998), p. 21.
21   Lee, H., *Elizabeth Bowen* (London, Vintage, 1999), p. 31.
22   Bowen, E., *Seven Winters*, op. cit. p. 7.
23   Bowen, E., *The Heat of the Day* (London, Cape, 1950), p. 155.
24   Bowen, E., *The Demon Lover and Other Stories* (London, Cape, 1947), p. 112.
25   Ibid. p. 95.
26   Glendinning, V. (ed.), *Elizabeth Bowen's Irish Stories* (Dublin, Poolbeg, 1978), p. 6.
27   Bowen, E., *The Demon Lover and Other Stories,* op. cit. p. 97
28   Ibid. p. 94.
29   Ibid. p. 109.
30   Ibid. p. 113